Profile
of
Theodore Roethke

CHARLES E. MERRILL PROFILES

Under the Editorship of
Matthew J. Bruccoli and Joseph Katz

Profile
of
Theodore Roethke

Compiled by
William Heyen
SUNY at Brockport

Charles E. Merrill Publishing Company
A Bell & Howell Company
Columbus, Ohio

ISBN: 0-675-09208-6

Library of Congress Catalog Card Number: 78-150129

1 2 3 4 5 6 7 8 9–76 75 74 73 72 71

Printed in the United States of America

Preface

Theodore Roethke (1908-1963) is increasingly being recognized as the finest American poet of his generation. From *Open House* (1941) to *The Far Field* (1964), his posthumous volume, he generated attention and excitement, if not unqualified praise. If his work is not consistently satisfying to individual readers, it is never boring. For Roethke felt the need to change his poetry as he himself changed, and from collection to collection his work demonstrates a remarkable range of voices, styles, and concerns. Where was Roethke at his best, and where did he fail?—perhaps these are the central questions posed by the contributors to this volume. The criticism collected here is not unanimous in its praise. The variety of Roethke's work challenges us to ask ourselves what we believe a poem must be and do.

I have brought together here what are, in my opinion, some of the most perceptive estimates of Roethke's achievement. I have leaned in my selection toward the substantial essay rather than toward bits and snippets from notes or reviews, and I have chosen material that is out of print or, in any case, not readily and conveniently available. Nine of the ten contributors to this volume are themselves poets, and the single exception, the late Allan Seager, was a novelist of distinction. Roethke has been luckier than most in having so many creative writers, the best of our critics, turn to his work, and this recognition is one indication of how deep his influence has been.

I have arranged the essays here not in the order in which they were first published, but, generally, according to the particular phase of Roethke's work with which they are concerned, from considerations of his earliest to his latest work. It may be that the reader of this collection, after becoming acquainted with Roethke's *Collected Poems* (1965), will want to go through these essays in order, or it may very well be that he will want to read the essays by Stanley Kunitz and James McMichael first, since these are overviews of Roethke's achievement.

W.H.

Contents

Chronicle of Events

1908   Theodore Huebner Roethke born on May 25, Saginaw, Michigan, the son of Otto Roethke and Helen Huebner.

1923   April, Otto Roethke dies.

1925-1929 Attends the University of Michigan, receives B.A.

1930-1931 Graduate study at Harvard.

1931-1935 Teaches and coaches tennis at Lafayette College; poems begin appearing regularly in periodicals.

1935   Teaches from end of September to mid-November at Michigan State University; has breakdown; hospitalized until January, 1936.

1936   Receives M.A. from University of Michigan; begins teaching at Pennsylvania State University and remains there until 1943.

1941   *Open House,* his first book, published.

1943-1946 Teaches at Bennington College; awarded Guggenheim fellowship in 1945.

1947   Begins teaching at the University of Washington.

1948   *The Lost Son and Other Poems.*

1950   Awarded second Guggenheim fellowship.

1951   *Praise to the End!*

1953   Marries Beatrice O'Connell; they travel in Europe from March until August; *The Waking: Poems 1933-1953* published.

1954   Receives Pulitzer Prize for *The Waking: Poems 1933-1953.*

1955-1956 Lectures in Italy under a Fulbright; travels to Spain, France, Austria, England; returns to United States in August, 1956.

1

1958   *Words for the Wind* published; awarded Bollingen Prize in Poetry of Yale University, and National Book Award.

1959   Awarded a two-year grant from Ford Foundation.

1960   Travels to Europe in June; enters hospital at Ballinisloe in August; spends winter in London.

1961   Returns to United States; *I Am! Says the Lamb* published.

1962   Awarded Honorary Doctor of Letters by University of Michigan; becomes Poet in Residence at University of Washington.

1963   *Party at the Zoo*, a children's book; *Sequence, Sometimes Metaphysical*; dies August 1.

1964   *The Far Field* published; wins National Book Award.

1966   *Collected Poems.*

Allan Seager, Stanley Kunitz, John Ciardi

An Evening with Ted Roethke

(The following discussion, by three of Theodore Roethke's old friends, took place on May 24, 1967, in Saginaw, Michigan, at the inauguration of The Theodore Roethke Memorial Foundation.)

ALLAN SEAGER: When we were talking this program over, I said that it might be a little too much to talk about Ted's boyhood in Saginaw since there are so many people here who knew about it. And then it was pointed out that this was a generation ago and there are a lot of people who might not know anything about it. Now, Ted's grandparents, as you probably know, came from Prussia, East Prussia, Pomerania. They settled here in 1872, about the time of the lumber boom, and his grandfather started a market garden, which was apparently needed, because things went very well. Ted's father and Ted's uncles worked in the garden, and eventually William Roethke made enough money to start a greenhouse. And that grew and prospered. At one time the Roethke greenhouses had more under glass than any greenhouses in the state.

Ted was born at 1805 Gratiot in 1908. Tomorrow would be his birthday. To those of you who knew him when he was full-grown, he wouldn't have presented the same picture as a child, because he was small, almost undersized, slender, and he was sickly. There was hardly a winter when he wasn't laid flat with what they used to call La Grippe. Probably flu. He had what is now an archaic operation, a mastoid operation. And he was sent, at the age of five, to the John Moore School. As many of you know, part of the curriculum there was the study of German, and Ted studied an hour of German a day from the time he went to school until he came to Arthur Hill High School. Yet he seemed to resist it. He never knew German really well, though he had a lot of half-profane idiomatic phrases he picked up from the gardeners in the greenhouse. But when he came to write his famous poem, "The Lost Son," there is a passage "Scurry of warm over small plants. Ordnung! Ordnung! Papa is coming!" Well, this is not what he meant in one sense. The proper German for "Look out! Look out!" would be "Achtung." And he admitted this later, "Ordnung" means "order." But, if you like, it was a Freudian slip, and it went better probably. Much later when Ted was at Yaddo with Robert Lowell and J. F. Powers, when he took too long in the bathroom, Lowell and Powers would beat on the door and say, "Ordnung! Ordnung! Papa is coming."

He went to the John Moore School and naturally came to this high school. And I asked one of his teachers at the John Moore School if he showed any precocity or brilliance. She said, "Oh, he was smart, but not any smarter than two or three others." And what was obvious about him when he was quite young was that he was a great reader, and he read far beyond his years, and at that time he could have had no notion of his own sensitivity.

When he came to Arthur Hill, he had desires to be an athlete. He played some second-string basketball, he played a little baseball, and he was out for track. He used to practice pole vaulting, a certain amount. Most of his contemporaries at Arthur Hill remember him as rather shy and diffident, and yet he made one of the illegal fraternities and . . . you see this was during prohibition, and I don't know—maybe someone in the audience could tell me— whether starting to drink was part of the initiation. But anyhow, it was . . . he started drinking in high school. He used to drink something called Saginaw Butch, which was sold, I believe, at a place called Butch Condinger's. And sometimes it was pink, apparently, sometimes it was white. And it cost three dollars for a quart Mason jar. Having come up through the same era, I wonder how he survived.

When he was thirteen, going on fourteen, I think the most important event of his whole life occurred to him. This was the death of his father. I believe all children see their parents as gods when they are very small, then they become demigods, and finally dwindle into human beings. Well, Otto Roethke died at the time he was to Ted a demigod. Ted had the usual sort of ambivalent relationship toward him of fear and adoration. Otto Roethke owned, along with his brother, Charles, four and a half acres out here, which they made into a kind of game preserve. Otto used to take Ted for walks, he used to take him down to Houghton Lake fishing, and he tried to make Ted into a kind of woodsman, and Ted appreciated this. But he was a man with a temper, and he often whacked Ted, and dying just at the age that Ted was, it made a terrific impression on him. His sister said that after the funeral Ted sat down at the head of the table and never left it from then on. He was head of the house.

But Otto Roethke remained a presence in Ted's mind throughout his life. Now the reason I say this is that I've read all of Ted's notebooks. He left 200 notebooks. What they used to call "two-bit notebooks" that you got out of the dime store. There's four stacks of them about this high [here Seager, seated at the speakers' table, leaned back in his chair and held his hand out sideways, shoulder high]. And the number of times his father occurs, in one connection or another, is constant. Hardly a week goes by he doesn't mention his father. And this lasted all his life. One of his last poems, as you know, was "Otto." When he made his great breakthrough in "The Lost Son," Ted is obviously the "lost son." He calls himself the protagonist, but he sees himself as Otto Roethke's son. And in Ted's mind, Otto Roethke sometimes became almost God. He says this flatly several times in his notes.

Now, Ted wanted to go to Harvard, but Harvard was in the Mysterious East and his mother didn't want him to go and . . . he said, "I'll work in a pickle factory first." And so he got a summer job for a couple of summers in the Heinz pickle factory, and he eventually became a sort of chief weigh-master, and he was always griping that the farmers would put the big cucumbers, the ones that were too big, really, for pickles, on the bottom and cover them up with little cucumbers.

Finally, he went to The University of Michigan. Now, apparently, he shot up during his seventeenth year, because there's a picture of him in Arthur Hill High School annual when he was about sixteen, and he's seated next to a couple of girls, and he's no bigger than they are. But, on his application to The University of Michigan, he was six feet one and a half and 195 pounds. He grew taller than that later.

At Ann Arbor, he studied literature mostly, and he bought a big raccoon coat. His first vacation—they said he used to hang around a drug store near the high school in his coat as a sign of his new estate as a college man. He had started to play tennis when he was about sixteen. He joined the canoe club here, and Mr. Morley told me that Ted would practice by the hour on a back-board. He was not especially talented as a tennis player, but his grandmother had a saying, *Mach es tüchtig*—"Do it right." And this is a common saying in the family, and apparently Pomeranians had a great sense of righteousness. Not moral righteousness, but just in doing things right. And I think Ted inherited this. It showed in the way he went at tennis, and it showed in the way he went at poetry. And he became a pretty good tennis player. He played in the state tournaments, and later on, he was tennis coach at Lafayette College and at Penn State College. Mr. Kunitz and he used to play for the World's Championship of Poets.

At Ann Arbor, he . . . I was in classes with him there, and he was again shy; he never said much. He joined the Chi Phi fraternity. He did quite a lot of drinking, one way or another. He wanted to write, but he didn't know what he wanted to write. His wife said, "Did you want to be a great poet?" And he said, "No, I wanted to be a great something." But he said he wanted to write a chiseled prose, and he bought all the O'Brien short-story annuals. He was going to write short stories because you can make money at it. He took his degree, and then he entered Law School. Now this seems to have been a family wish—perhaps his father had expressed some desire for this. He was in Law School at the same time as Judge Huff [the Honorable Eugene S. Huff, Circuit Court, Saginaw], and Judge Huff tells me that Ted used to come in at night and throw down his books, and curse the assignments of John Barker Waite. Ted was taking a course in criminal law. Well, he said he got a C in it, but—this is the terrible thing about having a biographer on your trail—I looked up his record. He got a D.

It was at some time in that year that he began to write poetry seriously. I'm inclined to think he began a little earlier, because I found scraps of poems in his undergraduate notebooks. He was a pack rat. He kept everything. He kept even his high-school papers, as well as most of his university papers. He kept all the notes he took in class, so it's not too hard to get a fairly good idea of how his mind worked, you see, from this vast mass of written material.

He got a job at Lafayette—the English Department had only four people in it at that time—and it was the policy to keep young men only two years. Well, they kept Ted four. I was down there talking to some people that had just seen the thirtieth reunion. And the people who had come back to the re-union, the only teacher they could remember in the whole college was Ted. He was a very vivid teacher, even then, and although he was supposed to be teaching argumentation, which, God knows, is one of the dullest aspects of English, he kept trying to bootleg literature into his classes. And he did. He also had a girl. He always had a girl every place he taught.

After he'd stayed four years there, he got a job at Michigan State. It was at Michigan State that he had his first mental episode. Now, Ted had an illness of a manic-depressive type. The manic periods were much longer than the depressive periods, and in his first semester there, he went to Mercywood Sanitarium and spent about a month, then came back to Saginaw, and he was not re-hired at Michigan State.

He was writing poetry very conscientiously by then, and at Ann Arbor he used to carry around with him a book of Eleanor Wiley's [sic] poetry. In the thirties, he was reading a great many lady poets. Emily Dickinson, Leonie Adams, Eleanor Wiley [sic], Louise Bogan. And Mr. Kunitz cautioned him about this. His manner was getting at times effeminate, which Ted certainly was not. By that time, he had achieved his full growth, and he once said when he was getting a job at Bennington, interviewing the President of Bennington, "I may look like a beer salesman, but I'm a poet." Ted did not fit the stereotype of the poet at all in his looks. And for him to be writing this kind of poetry, looking the way he did, there was a certain discrepancy.

The first working poet that he ever met was at Lafayette, Rolfe Humphries. Humphries had a summer place near there, and Ted met him, and used to spend a good deal of time with him, and Humphries read his things and criticized them. It was Humphries, I believe, who introduced him to Louise Bogan. Then one day he called on you, didn't he [Seager turned to Stanley Kunitz, seated at his right]. Mr. Kunitz had a place at New Hope, Pennsylvania, and he said Ted—in 1935—he said Ted came and banged on the door one day. He was quite shy, but he had some poetry with him. They became friends.

When he was writing the poems that went into his first book, *Open House,* he would very often send a poem to the three of them, Rolfe Humphries, Kunitz, and Miss Bogan, for their criticism. This is very sound, because he got expert criticism before he ever submitted it anyplace. Finally, he—I remember seeing a letter he wrote to Louise Bogan on his twenty-eighth birthday—he always thought his mind worked terribly slowly, and he said, "How little I have done. I'm twenty-eight, been writing poetry all this time, no book out." Very depressed. In 1942, he put out *Open House.* Now it didn't blow down the walls of Jericho, but it got good reviews, especially by W. H. Auden.

Ted had met Auden at Penn State when he came there to give a reading. In fact, Ted and Philip Shelley there were instrumental in getting Auden there, and Ted wanted to meet him. Ted was always measuring himself against contemporary poets. He knew that Auden had a terrific reputation at that time, and I think he wanted to see the man. He knew the poetry. And all his life long, he was sort of stacking himself up against whoever was writing poetry. He stayed at Penn State until about 1942, I think it was, and he went on leave and got a job at Bennington. He got me a job at Bennington for a year, and I was with him the year of 1944 and 1945 at Bennington. He had begun what are now called the "Greenhouse Poems." He had written several of them, and Kenneth Burke lived in the same house with him—the critic— and he wrote me and said, "I knew Ted's gong had struck when he hit that greenhouse line." Ted was trying definitely to break through into a new style.

There's a very strange thing happened. He was beginning work on "The Lost Son" in the fall of 1945. In his notebooks, there's the strange entry, "Why do I wish for an illness, something to get my teeth into." And, during the late autumn of 1945, his friends at Bennington could tell there was something the matter with him, and it was a second attack—he was winding up for it. And he was finally taken to Albany General Hospital, and he stayed there for about a month, and then he was in a nursing home for about a week or two, then he came back to Saginaw.

While he was, so to speak, well enough to be discharged, he was only partially stable. His sister was then teaching school, and she had to do all his typing, and he would keep her up half the night talking and typing and walking up and down. But he was working, he was finishing "The Lost Son" and finishing the poems that immediately followed this. He often said that when he came out of an episode, he was filled with new ideas and filled with energy. This is not to say that mental illness is an aid to poetry. I'm not saying that. And it did not happen again in precisely this way. This is one incident when some of his best work was done just immediately after he got out of the hospital. "The Lost Son" was recognized by all critics as a great poem.

start He felt that he had to go back to Penn State, because he was on leave. He went back for one semester, and then got a job at the University of Washington. Now, by this time, he had become, I think, probably, the greatest teacher of poetry in the country. There was a good deal of the ham in Ted. He was passionately involved with poetry himself, and he had a belief that all children are naturally creative and that their lives afterward stifle it, in most cases, and he believed it was his job to try and reach the creativity that had been there once. And I have seen him, at Bennington, take little girls that made debuts in New York—silly little girls—and, by sheer intensity, he would get beautiful poems out of them. I've never talked to a student of his that didn't feel—they always use the word "love"—they felt that he taught with love. He believed it, but he would do anything to get a good poem out of them. I had a student who was a student of Ted's, and I said, "How come you write such lousy short stories for me and such good poems for Ted?" And she said, "I'm afraid he'll hit me." There was this terrible intensity about his teaching.

At the University of Washington, he had not pupils, he had disciples. Elizabeth Bishop was teaching out there a year or so ago in the same room Ted used, and he had some bookshelves in the room, and on the underside of one of the shelves, written apparently with a nail file in the paint, it said, "Died, in an examination of Ted Roethke's, June so-and-so." He would very often give them, say, six nouns, and say, "All right, write three stanzas using these six nouns." This would be an examination. Well, they could do it by this time. He gave fiendishly difficult examinations, but he didn't think they were, you see. There was a place called the Rainbow Tavern near the University of Washington—they couldn't drink on the campus—so the tavern was a half mile away, I think, and Ted used to go down there after his afternoon classes and the class would just go on. I mean, it might go on until eleven

end o'clock at night.

When he was forty-five, he was giving a reading—he got a Ford Foundation fellowship, and he had been here in Saginaw all the summer and all the fall writing. I guess the money was burning a hole in his pocket, and he was going to give a reading on December 5th at the Poetry Center in New York, and he heard that Edith Sitwell, Dame Edith Sitwell, was in New York. She had praised him extravagantly in a book of hers, so Ted was beginning to get a little bit manic. He took a suite at the St. Regis. He told me later that "I was in my Aga Khan phase." He took a suite at the St. Regis where Miss Sitwell was staying. He called her up at two o'clock in the morning and asked her for a sleeping pill. She was charmed. She liked this.

Going across the street to the Poetry Center the night of his reading, Beatrice O'Connell, who was one of his former students at Bennington, caught up with him and said, "Hi. I bet you don't remember me." And he said, "Hi, chick, of course I do." He said, "Where can I get in touch with you?" And she said, "I didn't tell him my number," she said, "I'm in the book." She said, "I just wanted to see if he really did remember my name." And she said, "He called." Well, this was December 5th, the first time he had seen her since leaving Bennington, and a month later they were married. Auden stood best man and Louise Bogan matron of honor. Auden gave them the loan of his villa at Ischia, off the coast of Italy, near Naples. But Ted sort of dug his heels in. He didn't want to go. Beatrice, who had been abroad, talked him into it, and, when they got to Naples, Ted was not at all impressed by Vesuvius or the famous Bay, and said, "Let's just stay on the boat and ride around until it's time to go home." And she wheedled him ashore and got him settled in Auden's villa, and, once he was settled, he liked it all right.

But she tried to get him to learn Italian, and he kept hurling the book across the room. He couldn't get a taxi in Italian or French. He took three years of French in Ann Arbor. He took some Italian. He'd had eight years of German. When he went to Vienna he wrote a list of common nouns like "bread" and "beer," things he must have known. But he had this real resistance to foreign languages. When his poems started to be translated—there was a Frenchman named Alain Bosquet translated some poem of his which contains the word "killdeer." Well, you know a killdeer's a bird. But Bosquet didn't know that. So he read it as *assassin du cerf*, the "assassin of the stag," you see. Well, Ted was very fussy about it, but he didn't know enough about French to pick that up.

He suggested to Beatrice that she get a job. He said, "I can't respect you unless you work." While they were at Ischia, she was writing the Seattle School Board, and she got a job teaching French in the Seattle Schools and . . . I suffer from too much information. You see, what you must understand is, while I'm giving you this sort of run-down, is that he is writing poetry all the time. Just the sheer volume of work that you see in the notebooks and the dates—very often he dates them pretty accurately—there's hardly a day, whether he was sick or well, that he wasn't writing poetry.

Now, after "The Lost Son" he does something that . . . he writes lines of poetry rather than poems. He keeps saying over and over again, "What I need is themes." And he would write a line or two and draw a line under it, write another line or two and draw a line under it. Then maybe after five or six pages, you'd see him ring a line, then three or four pages more he'd ring another one. Then two or three notebooks away there would be eight or ten of the ringed lines written together. He always said he let the words suggest the poems. Well, very often some of his poems are mosaics of these single lines and there's hardly any syntactical connection between the lines. They might have been written months apart or even years apart.

Now, if you know a poem called "Elegy for Jane, My Student, Thrown by a Horse," there's a very vivid line in there, "a side-long pickerel smile." He wrote that in 1939, and he tried to work it into two or three poems in the 40's, and it finally comes to rest in this. The girl had been a student of his for one semester, and she had been thrown from a horse and killed. But she wasn't particularly well known to Ted, and this seems to be a formal elegy. Whether she had a side-long pickerel smile, God only knows. Then, a line in one of his most recent poems, which I'm going to read later. "The Meadow Mouse"–"The paralytic stunned in the tub, and the water rising"–that was written about 1937. There are many single lines that are very good. He constantly reread his notebooks, would pull them out, and they would appear in poems that were finished much later.

The main thing I want to leave with you is how hard he worked. Now, the very first poem he ever wrote he got a dollar for from some little magazine that is now dead. I say this to encourage any poets in the audience. He said himself, "My first verses, and dreadful they were." Well, his first poem was two lines–first published poem:

> Sweep up the broken dreams of youth.
> The broom to use is utter truth.

That's terrible. And as I say, Ted said once in his notes, "the only death is the death of the will." His whole career as a poet seems to have been an act of will. He was a tremendously hard worker. He sacrificed himself and people to become the poet that is now in this book.

STANLEY KUNITZ: I thought I knew a lot about Ted, but I've learned a lot sitting beside Allan Seager this evening. I keep thinking how much Ted would have relished this occasion. He would have gloried in it. He was never one to be guilty of false modesty. He always ranked himself among the really great, and he had reason to. And I think that at the same time he would have griped a little, he would have said, "Well now, where's Auden tonight? What about Lowell? What about that chump Robert Graves? Why aren't they all here? They should be around." That's exactly, I'm sure, the way he would have felt. And at the same time, he would have been terribly embarrassed by the whole event. I recall a sentence that I copied out from one of his notebooks: "I always wonder, when I'm on the podium, why I am there. I really belong in some dingy pool hall under the table." And I think that all these reactions give you some sense of the man.

Of course, he's terribly important to me as he is to many others. He was, above all, to me, the poet of my generation who meant most, both in his person and in his art. For me to say, in fact, a poet of my generation, is to name him. Immediately after Eliot and Pound, and Hart Crane and Stevens and William Carlos Williams, to mention only a handful, it was difficult to be taken seriously as a new American poet. For the title to the new poetry was in possession of a dynasty of extraordinary gifts and powers, not the least of which was its stubborn capacity for survival. These poets would never consent to die. It is amazing—their longevity.

When Roethke was a schoolboy, in Michigan in the 20's, these poets, born late in the nineteenth century, had already arrived with a bang. For a long time, in the general view, they remained the rebels and inventors beyond whom most college courses in contemporary literature scarcely dared to venture. Of course, that's changing now. But up to a few years ago, this was preëminently true. Roethke took his own work seriously indeed. Lashed by his competitive and compulsive temper, he committed himself fully to the exhausting struggle for recognition—a desperately intimate struggle that left its mark on him.

Not so many years before his death, he could refer to himself sardonically as the oldest younger poet in the U.S.A. America tends to wither its artists with neglect or kill them with success. When recognition came to Roethke, it came in full measure except for the seductive blessing of a mass audience. He won the Pulitzer Prize in 1954 for *The Waking*. In 1959, after the publication of *Words for the Wind*, his collected verse, he received eight awards in all, including some prizes, grants, and honors that nobody had ever heard of before—or since, in fact. The flattery that meant most of all came in the form of imitation by dozens of even younger poets, including some with gray hair. Ted would occasionally make a fuss about these pretenders who were, as he said, stealing his stuff. I think you've all heard that phrase of his. One did not take the complaints at face value.

More than thirty years have passed since he blew into my life like the "big wind" of one of his poems. I was living in the Delaware Valley then. He came, unannounced, downriver from Lafayette College, where he was instructor in English, and, more satisfying to his pride, tennis coach. My recollection is of a traditionally battered jalopy from which a perfectly tremendous raccoon coat emerged. I'm sure it was the same coat that you have mentioned [turning to

Seager]. With my first book of poems tucked under its left paw, the introductory mumble that followed could be construed as a compliment. Then he stood, embarrassed and inarticulate in my doorway waiting to gauge the extent of my hospitality. The image that never left me was of a blond, smooth, shambling giant, irrevocably Teutonic, with a cold pudding of a face, somehow contradicted by the sullen down-turn of the mouth and the pale furious eyes—a countenance ready to be touched by time, waiting to be transfigured with a few subtle lines into a tragic mask. He had come to talk about poetry and talk we did over a jug of booze, grandly and vehemently all through the night.

There were occasions through the years that followed when I could swear that I hadn't been to bed since. All those evenings seemed to move inexorably towards a moment of trial for both of us. When he would fumble for the crinkled manuscript in his pocket, which, as we know, he had already presented to—at least two others—had presented for approval. During the reading of his poem, he waited in an attitude of excruciating tension and suspicion. If the praise failed to meet his expectation, he would grow violently defensive or lapse into a hostile silence. These poems were terribly important to him.

Nevertheless, he was by no means impervious to criticism or to suggestions. When I proposed "Open House" as the title for his first book of poems, published in 1941, he not only adopted it gratefully but proceeded to write the title poem that still stands at the head of his collected verse, the poem that begins, under the title "Open House":

> My secrets cry aloud.
> I have no need for tongue.
> My heart keeps open house,
> My doors are widely swung.
> An epic of the eyes
> My love, with no disguise.

On another country visit, perhaps a decade later, he asked me, long after midnight—we were sitting up again—to read something choice to him. I picked up Sir John Davies' neglected Elizabethan masterpiece, "Orchestra," a poem that he had somehow never chanced on, despite his omniverous appetite for verse, and I can still recall the excitement with which he responded to the clear voice of music. From that encounter, combined with his deep attachment to the beat of Yeats—it was beat, above all, that enchanted him— he composed a memorable sequence, "Four for Sir John Davies," which was to set the cadence for a whole new cycle of later poems.

> Is that dance slowing in the mind of man
> That made him think the universe could hum?

> The great wheel turns its axle when it can;
> I need a place to sing, and dancing-room,
> And I have made a promise to my ears
> I'll sing and whistle romping with the bears.

Ted wasn't easy on his friends, but neither was he easy on himself. For a while, when our dialogue arrived at an impasse, we could always fight it out on the tennis courts. What we liked to boast, as you've already indicated, [again, directed to Seager], with a bow to Joyce, was a "Lawn—Tennyson Championship of the World of Poetry." For all his six foot three, two-hundred-plus pound bulk and his lumbering gait, he was amazingly nimble on his feet. And, less amazingly, ruthless at the kill, with a smashing service and a tremendous forehand drive. The demon in him played the game just as it wrote the poems. Whatever he did was an aspect of the same insatiable will to conquer self and art and others. He could not bear to lose. If you managed to beat him, by cunning and by luck, you could not expect to be congratulated by him. He never leaped over the net and shook your hand. He was more likely to smash his racket across his knees, because I've seen him do it. After the steady deterioration of his body had forced him to abandon the game—his knees in particular gave out—he retreated into croquet and badminton, which he played with the same rapture and *fröhlichkeit*.

As a young man, he felt humiliated and disgraced by the periodic mental breakdowns that were to afflict him all his life. There were outbreaks and absences and silences that he had to cover up, partly because he realized what a threat they offered to his survival in the academic world. He was one of the supreme teachers of poetry, as his students have testified. But not until he came, after Bennington, to the University of Washington, in 1947, did he have any assurance of tenure. There he found a staunch advocate in the person of Robert Heilman, Chairman of the English Department, who remained loyal to him through the worst of weathers. I think all lovers of poetry owe a debt to Bob Heilman.

By the time of his arrival in Seattle, Roethke had found the means of transforming his ordeal into language; notably, in the unfettered masterful sequence of longer poems, initiated by "The Lost Son." Eventually, he more than half believed that the springs of his disorder were inseparable from the sources of his art, and he could brag, as he did in some of his late poems, of belonging to the brotherhood of mad poets that includes William Blake, John Clare, and Christopher Smart, with each of whom he was able to identify himself as lost. His affection for Dylan Thomas had much the same base, but, on the other hand, some of his longest friendships, including those with Louise Bogan and Wystan Auden, signified his unswerving admiration for those who stood in his mind as representatives of a sacred discipline.

[What I wrote in the magazine, *Poetry*, about *The Lost Son*, on its publication in 1948—this is a book of his that I continue to think of as a great one, or at least the central great one—still sounds pertinent to me. "The ferocity of Roethke's imagination makes most contemporary poetry seem pale and tepid in contrast. Even the wit is murderous. What Roethke brings us is news of the root, of the minimum, of the primordial. The sub-human is given tongue and the tongue proclaims the agony of coming alive. The painful miracle of growth."

Let me add now that one of Roethke's remarkable powers, particularly evident in the later productions, is that of the compassionate flow of self into the things of his experience. His poems become what they love; and mostly, he loves the creature-world, smaller and purer than his own] I quote now from one of his poems ["The Minimal," opening lines] :

> I study the lives on a leaf: the little
> Sleepers, numb nudgers in cold dimensions,
> Beetles in caves, newts, stone-deaf fishes,
> Lice tethered to long limp subterranean weeds,
> Squirmers in bogs,
> And bacterial creepers . . . .

No other modern poet seems so directly tuned to the natural universe. His disturbance was in being human. The soul trapped in his earthen frame yearned less for the infinite than for the infinitesimal. This florist's son never really departed from the moist fecund world of his father's greenhouse here in Saginaw.] In "Cuttings," one of a bouquet of greenhouse poems, he gives a clue to his root image:

> This urge, wrestle, resurrection of dry sticks,
> Cut stems struggling to put down feet,
> What saint strained so much,
> Rose on such lopped limbs to a new life?
>
> I can hear, underground, that sucking and sobbing,
> In my veins, in my bones I feel it,
> The small waters seeping upward,
> The tight grains parting at last.
> When sprouts break out, slippery as fish,
> I quail, lean to beginnings, sheath-wet.

[He is our poet of transformations, and his imagination is populated with shape-shifters who are aspects of his own being, driven to know itself and yet appalled by the terrible necessity of self-knowledge. The life in his poems emerges out of stones and swamps, tries on leaves and wings, struggles toward the divine. Brooding on God, he wrote towards the end, "I may become a man." He could turn even his stammerings into art. ⌉ ~End~

In 1953, as you've already been told, Roethke married one of his former Bennington students, Beatrice O'Connell, to whom he was to address dozens of love poems—a sort of serial epithalamium, including the dazzling verses that begin, "I knew a woman lovely in her bones." During their weekend visit after their wedding, I prodded him to write an autobiographical sketch for the first supplement to *Twentieth-Century Authors,* a reference work that I was editing. The resulting document in longhand, still in my possession, provides an invaluable insight into his creative intentions. One much quoted passage reads: "I have tried to transmute and purify my life, the sense of being defiled by it, in both small and formal and somewhat blunt short poems, and latterly in longer poems which try in their rhythms to catch the very movement of the mind itself, to trace the spiritual history of a protagonist. Not I, personally, but all haunted and harried men, to make in this series a true and not arbitrary order, which will permit many ranges of feeling including him."

He ranged so far that he found it possible increasingly to incorporate a wild sort of laughter into his flights. Indeed, though he was brother to the mad poets, and felt his kinship with all haunted and harried men, he had an inordinate capacity for joy. "I count myself among the happy poets," he could say, knowing that the laughter and the fierceness and the terror were indivisible. In this matter of making noise that rhymes—his phrase—he dared to seek a combination of vulgarity and nobility. And he put his stamp on the mixture. He was not to be admired as a vessel of decorum. After all, one doesn't go to the axe to learn about politeness. In his world of sensibility, ribaldry, rage, and tenderness coexisted.

Nobody since Edward Lear, I'm convinced, has composed such hilarious verses for children. It was during the wedding visit that he proposed to demonstate his comic genius by entertaining my three-year-old daughter with recitation of his nonsense verse. His first selection was a quatrain entitled, "The Cow." Dancing around her, thumping out the beat, illustrating the action with appropriate gestures, he roared the lines:

> There once was a cow with a double udder.
> When I think of it now, I just have to shudder.
> She was too much for one, You can bet your life.
> She had to be milked by a man and his wife.

The result might have been anticipated. Gretchen burst into tears and tried to hide under the sofa.

I was to think of that incident seven years later, in the spring of 1960, when Roethke read at the Poetry Centre in New York, where I introduced him. He had a high fever, and backstage he was jittery, sweating copiously from every pore as he guzzled champagne—"bubbly," as he liked to call it. It was his last reading in New York. On stage for the first portion of his program, he clowned and hammed incorrigibly, weaving, gyrating, dancing, shrugging his shoulders, muttering to himself intermittently, and now and then making curiously flipper-like or foetal gestures with his hands. But gradually, as the evening wore on, he settled into a straight dramatic style that was enormously effective and moving. When it came to his new mad sequence, headed by the poem that begins "In a dark time, the eye begins to see," his voice rang out with such an overwhelming roll of noble anguish that there were many in the audience who wept. As we filed out of the hall, a friend of mine remarked on Roethke's strange affinity to that other lost and violent spirit, the artist, Jackson Pollock. How true. I thought. And I heard myself repeating a rather enigmatic phrase that I'd picked up from the painter, Franz Klein, when he was reminiscing to me about his late companion, Pollock. And what he said was, "He divined himself." And I think that's very true about Ted Roethke. Thank You.

JOHN CIARDI: I think one of the things Roethke would have liked most about this evening is the simple fact that Stanley Kunitz is here. I met Roethke when I was, I think, a late junior or an early senior, as an undergraduate. My teacher at Tufts University, John Holmes, had taught at Lafayette with Roethke, and Roethke came by to visit him. I remember we were walking down fraternity row when John said he was a member of ATO and Ted turned to me and said, "What's your fraternity." And I said, "NYA." He reminded me of that some time later.

I had been reading Roethke's poems because he sent copies to John Holmes. At that time, I thought of him as a marvelous jewel worker, who forms an open house of the precise and beautifully lapidary descriptions of a heron standing on one foot in a Michigan swamp, or of a highway with something terrible about to happen. These things were drawn like cameos, and impressively, so. But also, at the same time, Roethke was enormously excited about Stanley Kunitz's book, *Intellectual Things.* Certainly there was a real flow of spirit back and forth between the two that suddenly has added to both of them. I think there's a rightness, a fitness to that.

As Mr. Seager was talking about the wedding, I recalled an incident that I think will do as an illustration. We're here, in a sense, to memorialize a man, and the poet creates a personality. It's one of the things he does. His work leaves for all time a personality that wasn't there before. There's always the

danger that we will identify a biographical personality with the personality
the poet creates. And that isn't so. I don't know whether I would have liked
John Donne or not, but there is a personality called "John Donne." I know I
certainly did love Theodore Roethke, when I wasn't being overwhelmed by
him, but that certainly is not the personality of the poems.

But the day he got married—it was a Saturday, as I recall—and the phone
rang at about eleven o'clock, when we were having a party in Boston at that
time and he was getting married in New York. And I said, "Hello." And he
said, "Well, hello, my blankety-blank, you ginzo blankety-blank, this is your
uncle Ted." And I said, "Ted, what are you doing?" And he said, "I'm getting
married, what in hell do you think I'm doing?" And this went on, and he
said, "Now look. If you want to get your skin full of hooch, you get on a
plane and get down here." Well, I made the stupid apologies you have to; we
had company coming—I don't think I had the plane fare, as a matter of
fact—there were all these problems. But finally he switched to something
else—and I think this was typical of Ted, his marvellous delusions of grandeur
at times—he said, "Well, I tell you. You know all those syndicate boys up in
Boston don't you?" And I said, "Who? Me?" But he collected gangsters. He
loved to tell stories about them and the horrible things they did. And when
he couldn't tell stories about them, he'd invent them. But this was part of a
stage personality that gave him pleasure. Well, I finally convinced him that I
was not on intimate terms with the Boston syndicate. And he assumed that
with a name like Ciardi, I had to be in the Mafia or something. I was to send
him all of the Boston underworld. I was working for a publisher at the time
and we had done a dictionary of underworld lingo compiled in one of the
prisons in New York. And he said, "Well, I'll let you off the hook if you'll
send me that dictionary of underworld lingo." So I sent him the dictionary of
underworld lingo, and whatever it was was saved.

Then, as has been mentioned, there was the enormously competitive, compulsive athlete. But it was forever a complex personality. At Yaddo one
summer—I guess I was eight or nine years younger than Roethke, and a little
more agile than I am now—he decided that we were going to go out on the
field and he was going to bat balls over my head. There was a pine wood
behind us, and he would keep batting the balls out and I would race back and
catch them, and he would take a mightier swing yet, and I would race back
and catch them. And every time I caught one he began to howl, "God damn
it, can't you drop one?" He was going to send one over my head. And finally
he hit one right into the pine woods, and I ran in and grabbed a branch and
swung up and caught the thing. And I heard a yowl, and I turned around.
He'd disappeared, but the bat was still up in the air. He'd gone off through
the bushes. I didn't see him until about eight o'clock that night, and he came
tap-tapping at the door with a tray and a bottle of brandy and two glasses and

a sweet smile on his face and not a word said. It was the marvellous complexity of the man.

But I don't think that's the man of the poems. It's there in some of them, you know, "O what's the weather in a Beard" and in the boisterousness. I have to feel that these were partly outbursts of energy and partly defenses. That the real creation is a voice inside of all of these things that sings out of the poems. There was that facing of the boisterousness. He liked to play Paul Bunyan. But when he sat down in the real silence of himself, it was the really made personality that came out . . . .

Kenneth Burke

The Vegetal Radicalism of Theodore Roethke

Perhaps the best way-in is through the thirteen flower poems that comprise the first section of *The Lost Son*. The two opening lyrics, "Cuttings" and "Cuttings (Later)," present the vital strivings of coronated stem, severed from parental stock. Clearly the imagistic figuring of a human situation, they view minutely the action of vegetal "sticks-in-a drowse" as

> One nub of growth
> Nudges a sand-crumb loose,
> Pokes through a musty sheath
> Its pale tendrilous horn.

The second of the two (that sum up the design of this particular poetic vocation) should be cited entire, for its nature as epitome:

> This urge, wrestle, resurrection of dry sticks,
> Cut stems struggling to put down feet,
> What saint strained so much,
> Rose on such lopped limbs to a new life?

From *Language as Symbolic Action* (Berkeley and Los Angeles: The University of California Press, 1966), pp. 254-81. Reprinted by permission of the author and The Regents of the University of California. Originally published in *The Sewanee Review*, LVIII (January 1950), 68-108.

> I can hear, underground, that sucking and sobbing,
> In my veins, in my bones I feel it,—
> The small waters seeping upward,
> The tight grains parting at last.
> What sprouts break out,
> Slippery as fish,
> I quail, lean to beginnings, sheath-wet.

Severedness, dying that is at the same time a fanatic tenacity; submergence (fish, and the sheer mindless nerves of sensitive plants); envagination as a homecoming.

To characterize the others briefly: "Root Cellar" (of bulbs that "broke out of boxes hunting for chinks in the dark," of shoots "lolling obscenely," of roots "ripe as old bait"—a "congress of stinks"); "Forcing House" (a frantic urgency of growth, "shooting up lime and dung and ground bones" . . . "as the live heat billows from pipes and pots"); "Weed Puller" (the poet "Under the concrete benches, / Hacking at black hairy roots,— / Those lewd monkey-tails hanging from drainholes"); "Orchids" ("adder-mouthed" in the day, at night "Loose ghostly mouths / Breathing"); "Moss-Gathering" (the guilt of moss-gathering); "Old Florist" (genre portrait, lines in praise of a man vowed to the ethics of this vegetal radicalism); "Transplanting" (a companion piece to the previous poem, detailing *operations* in ways that appeal to our *sensations*); "Child on Top of a Greenhouse" (the great stir below, while the young hero climbs, smashing through glass, the wind billowing out the seat of his britches); "Flower-Dump" (the picturesqueness greatly increased by a strong contrast, as the catalogue of the heap and clutter ends on a vision of "one tulip on top / One swaggering head / Over the dying, the newly dead"); "Carnations" (where the theme shifts to talk of "a crisp hyacinthine coolness, / Like that clear autumnal weather of eternity,"—a kind of expression, as we shall later try to indicate, not wholly characteristic of this poet).

From this group we omitted one item, "Big Wind," because we want to consider it at greater length. It reveals most clearly how Roethke can endow his brief lyrics with intensity of *action*. Nor is the effect got, as so often in short forms, merely by a new spurt in the last line. No matter how brief the poems are, they progress from stage to stage. Reading them, you have strongly the sense of entering at one place, winding through a series of internal developments, and coming out somewhere else. Thus "Big Wind" first defines the situation (water shortage in greenhouse during storm) with a five-line rhetorical question. Next come fifteen lines describing the action appropriate to the scene, the strained efforts of those who contrive to keep the pipes supplied with hot steam. Then the substance of this account is restated in a figure that likens the hothouse to a ship riding a gale. And after eleven lines amplifying the one turbulent metaphor, there are two final lines wherein the agitation subsides into calm, with a splendid gesture of assertion. We cite the summarizing image, and its closing couplet:

> But she rode it out,
> That old rose-house,
> She hove into the teeth of it,
> The core and pith of that ugly storm,
> Ploughing with her stiff prow,
> Bucking into the wind-waves
> That broke over the whole of her,
> Flailing her sides with spray,
> Flinging long strings of wet across the roof-top,
> Finally veering, wearing themselves out, merely
> Whistling thinly under the wind-vents;
> She sailed until the calm morning,
> Carrying her full cargo of roses.

The unwinding of the trope is particularly fortunate in suggesting transcendence because the reference to the "full cargo of roses," even as we are thinking of a ship, suddenly brings before us a vision of the greenhouse solidly grounded on *terra firma*; and this shift apparently helps to give the close its great finality. Thus, though you'd never look to Roethke for the rationalistic, the expository steps are here ticked off as strictly as in the successive steps of a well-formed argument. And thanks to the developmental structure of such poems, one never thinks of them sheerly as descriptive: they have the vigor, and the poetic morality, of action, of form unfolding.

To round out this general sampling, we might consider a poem written since the publication of *The Lost Son*. It is "The Visitant," and in contrast with "The Big Wind," which is robust, it possesses an undulance, a hushedness, a contemplative, or even devotional attitude, that makes of love an almost mystic presence. Roethke here begins with such a natural scene as would require a local deity, a *genius loci,* to make it complete. Hence as the poem opens, the place described is infused with a *numen* or *pneuma*, a concentration of spirit just on the verge of apparition.

The work is divided into three movements: the first anticipatory, the third reminiscent, the second leading through a partly secular, yet gently pious, theophany. The mood is beautifully sustained.

The introductory stanza evokes a secretive spot by a stream, at a time of vigil ("I waited, alert as a dog") while, with a shift in the slight wind (figuring also a breath of passion?), "a tree swayed over water." Nine lines establishing expectancy, a state of suspension as though holding one's breath. ("The leech clinging to a stone waited.")

The second stanza is of the "coming." We quote it entire:

Slow, slow as a fish she came,
Slow as a fish coming forward,
Swaying in a long wave;
Her skirts not touching a leaf,
Her white arms reaching toward me.

She came without sound,
Without brushing the wet stones;
In the soft dark of early evening,
She came,
The wind in her hair,
The moon beginning.

The wind is thus there too, so the ambiguities of the advent may now presumably stand also for erotic movements sometimes celebrated by poets as a "dying." The swaying tree of the first stanza has its counterpart in the swaying "fish" of the second.

The third stanza is of the same scene, now retrospectively: The spirit is there still, but only through having been there, as in the first stanza it was there prophetically. Thus, at the end:

A wind stirred in a web of appleworms;
The tree, the close willow, swayed.

The peculiar mixture of tension and calm in this poem is of great felicity. The talk of "swaying," the key word repeated in each stanza, has its replica in the cradle-like rhythm. And the whole effect is gratifyingly idyllic, even worshipful.

As a comment on method, we might contrast "The Visitant" with another poem where Roethke was apparently attempting, in a somewhat "essayistic" manner, to trace the birth of Psyche. It begins

The soul stirs in its damp folds,
Stirs as a blossom stirs,
Still wet from its bud-sheath,
Slowly unfolding.

Cyclamen, turtle, minnow, child, seed, snail—each in turn is exploited to define how the spirit moves, "still and inward." The lines are the poet's *De Anima*: and the emergent soul is seen ultimately in terms of an inner Snail-Phallus. As there is a mind's eye, a spirit breath, an inner ear, so he would seem to conceive a kind of transcendent sex-within-sex, the essence of pure snailhood ("outward and inward" . . . "hugging a rock, stone and horn" . . . "taking and embracing its surroundings"). But though the poem is almost a review of Roethke's favorite images, it is far less successful in combining Psyche and Eros than "The Visitant." For it is weaker in action, development, being rather a series of repetitive attempts to arrive at the same end from different images as starting point. Roethke could have got to this poem by translating the theories of mystical theology directly into his own impressionistic equivalent. In "The Visitant" he has moved beyond such mere correspondences by introducing a dramatic situation and building around it. A comparison of the two poems shows how the essayistic (that moves toward excellence in Pope) could be but an obstruction to Roethke.[1]

We have said that the mention of "coolness" and "eternity" was not characteristic of Roethke's language. We meant this statement in the strictest sense. We meant that you will rarely find in his verse a noun ending in "-ness" or "-ity." He goes as far as is humanly possible in quest of a speech wholly devoid of abstractions.

To make our point by antithesis: glancing through Eliot's "Burnt Norton," we find these words:

abstraction, possibility, speculation, purpose, deception, circulation, arrest, movement, fixity, freedom, compulsion, *Erhebung* without motion, concentration without elimination, completion, ecstasy, resolution, enchantment, weakness, mankind, damnation, consciousness, disaffection, stillness, beauty, rotation, permanence, deprivation, affection, plentitude, vacancy, distraction, apathy, concentration, eructation, solitude, darkness, deprivation, destitution, property, dessication, evacuation, inoperancy, abstention, appetency, silence, stillness, co-existence, tension, imprecision, temptation, limitation.

If Roethke adheres to his present aesthetic, there are more of such expressions in this one Quartet of Eliot's than Roethke's Vegetal Radicalism would require for a whole lifetime of poetizing.

In one poem, to be sure, they do cluster. In "Dolor," lines detailing the "tedium" of "institutions" (notably the schoolroom), we find, besides these two words: sadness, misery, desolation, reception, pathos, ritual, duplication. But their relative profusion here explains their absence elsewhere, in verse written under an aesthetic diametrically opposed to such motives. (In one place he uses "sweetness" as a term of endearment, yet the effect is more like an epithet than like an abstract noun.)

Accordingly, in the attempt to characterize Roethke's verse, you could

---

[1] Since this comment was written, the poem has been greatly revised, mainly by omission of about half its original contents. In its final form, there is a progression of but three images (blossom, minnow, snail) culminating in a catachresis ("music in a hood"). One epithet ("a light breather") is lifted from the body of the poem to be used as title. And the last six lines diminish gradually from ten syllables to two. The poem has thus finally been assimilated, has been made developmental.

profitably start from considerations of vocabulary. The motive that we have in mind is by no means peculiar to this one poet. It runs through modern art generally. And though few of the artists working in this mode are interested in formal philosophy, the ultimate statement of the problem would take us back to some basic distinctions in Immanuel Kant's *Critique of Pure Reason*: notably his way of aligning "intuitions," "concepts," and "ideas."

If you perceive various sensations (of color, texture, size, shape, etc.), you are experiencing what Kant would call "intuitions of sensibility." If you can next "unify" this "manifold" (as were you to decide that the entire lot should be called a "tree"), in this word or name you have employed a "concept of the understanding." "Intuitions" and "concepts," taken together, would thus sum up the world of visible, tangible, audible things, the objects and operations of our sensory experience. And because of their positive, empirical nature, they would also present the sensible material that forms the basis of a poetic image (however "spiritual" may be the implications of the poet's language in its outer reaches).

"Intuitions" and "concepts" belong to Kant's "Aesthetic" and "Analytic" respectively. But there is also a purely "Dialectical" realm, comprising "ideas of reason." This is the world of such invisible, intangible, inaudible things as "principles." The various "isms" would be classed as "ideas of reason." In carrying out an idea, men will at every turn deal with the concrete objects that are represented in terms of "intuitions" and "concepts"; yet the idea itself is not thus "empirical," but purely "dialectical," not available to our senses alone, or to measurement by scientific instruments.

Do not these distinctions of Kant's indicate the direction which poetry might take, in looking for a notable purification of language? If one could avoid the terms for "ideas," and could use "concepts" only insofar as they are needed to unify the manifold of "intuitions," the resultant vocabulary would move toward childlike simplicity. And it would be cleansed of such unwieldly expressions (now wielded by politicos and journalists) as: capitalism, fascism, socialism, communism, democracy (words unthinkable in Roethke's verse, which features rather: cry, moon, stones, drip, toad, bones, snail, fish, flower, house, water, spider, pit, dance, kiss, bud, sheath, bud-sheath, ooze, slip-ooze, behind which last term, despite ourselves, we irresponsibly keep hearing a child's pronunciation of "slippers").

Kant's alignment was designed primarily to meet the positivistic requirements of modern technological science. And since he himself, in the *Critique of Judgment,* talked of "aesthetic ideas," the issue is not drawn by him with finality. The modern lyric poet of imagistic cast might even with some justice think of himself as paralleling the scientific ideal, when he stresses the vocabulary of concrete things and sensible operations; yet the typical scientist language, with its artificially constructed Greek-Roman compounds, seems usable only in a few sophisticated gestures (as with the ironic nostalgia of a Laforgue). This much is certain, however: Whatever the complications, we can use the Kantian distinctions to specify a possible criterion for a purified poetic idiom. The ideal formula might be stated thus: *A minimum of "ideas," a maximum of "intuitions."* In this form, it can sum up the Roethkean aesthetic. (The concept would be admitted as a kind of regrettable necessity.)

For further placements (as regards the problems of linguistic purity set by urbanization), we might think of Dante's *De Vulgari Eloquentia*, Wordsworth's Preface to the *Lyrical Ballads*, and D. H. Lawrence's cult of the "physical" as contrasted with the "abstract."

Dante introduced the criterion of the *infantile* in the search for a purified poetic idiom. Choosing between learned Latin and the vernacular, he noted that the "vulgar locution" which infants imitate from their nurses is "natural" and "more noble," hence the most fit for poetry. But though he set up the infantile as a criterion for preferring Italian to a learned and "artificial" langauge, his criteria for the selection of a poetic vocabulary within Italian itself encompassed a quite mature medium. Thus, the ideal speech should be "illustrious, cardinal, courtly, and curial"; and in such a language, one would necessarily introduce, without irony or sullenness, many "ideas of reason." Indeed, what we have called the "infantile" criterion of selection we might rather call a search for the ideal mother tongue (had it not been for the Fall, Dante reminds us, all men would still speak Hebrew, the language of the Garden of Eden). That is, we could stress its *perfection,* its maturity and scope (its "mother wit"), rather than its *intellectual limitations* (though in the first great division of labor, separating those who specialize in being males and those who specialize in being females, the class of womanhood would seem to be the "more noble," so far as concerned its associations with the *medium* of poetry). The ideal language, we might say, was under the sign not of the child but of the Virgin Mother; though even, had the infant Jesus been the ultimate term for the motivation here, his essential kingliness would have been enough to derive the illustrious, cardinal, courtly, and curial from the infantile alone, as so modified.

In any case, as early as Dante's time, though prior to the upsurge of the industrial revolution, the division of labor was sufficiently advanced for him to assert that each kind of craftsman had come to speak a different language in the confusion of tongues caused during work on the Tower. The diversity of languages was thus derived from specialization, quite as with particular technical idioms today—and the higher the specialized activity, Dante says, the more "barbarous" its speech. His principle of selection could thus acquire a new poignancy later, when the learned language he had rejected had become an essential part of the vernacular itself, and when the relation between mother and child is not formally summed up in the infancy of a universal ruler (though, roundabout, in furtive ways, there are the modern mothers who are by implication ennobled, in giving birth to offspring they encourage to be child-tyrants).

By the time of Wordsworth's preface, after several centuries of progressively accelerated industrialization, the search for a principle of selection, for a "purified" speech, involves another kind of regression, a romantic reversion, not just to childhood simplicity, but also to "low and rustic life." For in this condition, "the essential passions of the heart . . . can attain their maturity, are less under restraint, and speak a plainer and more emphatic language." Though Wordsworth is talking of the rustic life itself, approaching the problem in terms of language (as Wordsworth's own explicit concern with selection entitles us to do), we should stress rather the *imagery* drawn from "the necessary character of rural occupations." Such imagery, he says, would be "more easily comprehended" and "more durable"; and by it "our elementary feelings" would be "more forcibly communicated," since "the passions of men are incorporated with the beautiful and permanent forms of nature."

Wordsworth is also explicitly considering another threat to poetry, the journalistic idiom which by now has almost become the norm with us, so that poets are repeatedly rebuked for not writing in a style designed to be used once and thrown away. Thus, on the subject of the causes that now act "with a combined force to blunt the discriminating powers of the mind," bringing about "a state of almost savage stupor," Wordsworth writes:

> The most effective of these causes are the great national events which are daily taking place, and the increasing accumulation of men in cities, where the uniformity of their occupations produces a craving for extraordinary incident, which the rapid communication of intelligence hourly gratifies.

"The rapid communication of intelligence hourly"; this is Wordsworth's resonant equivalent for "journalism." In such an expression he does well by it, even while recognizing its threat to poetic purity as he conceives of such purity.

He goes on to state his belief that, despite his preference for the ways of pretechnological nature as the basis for a poet's imagery, "If the time should ever come when what is now called Science . . . shall be ready to put on . . . a form of flesh and blood, the Poet will lend his divine spirit to aid the transfiguration." Maybe yes, maybe no. Though concerned with the purification of vocabulary for poetic purposes, Wordsworth does not show (or even ask) how the technological idioms themselves can be likened to the language learned at the breast.

We should note, however, one major respect in which the terms of the new technology are in spirit a language close to childhood. For they have the quality of death rays and rocket ships, and other magical powers the thought of which can make the child wonder and in his imagination feel mighty. Indeed, the pageantry of the technological (the new lore of the giant-killers) can appeal to the infantile, long before there is any concern with such romances of love as, variously, concern Dante, Wordsworth, and Roethke, all three. What you put around a Christmas tree reflects no longer the mystery of the Birth, but the wonders of modern technological production. So, surprisingly, we glimpse how a poet's nursery language may be more mature than at first it may seem. It may be no younger than the adolescent in spirit, though this adolescence is on the side that leans toward the universal sensibility of childhood (and of the maternal) rather than toward the forensic, abstract, and journalistically "global."

A bridge-builder, no matter how special his language, has successfully "communicated" with his fellows when he has built them a good bridge. In this respect, the languages of the technological specialties confront a different communicative problem than marks the language of the specialist in verse. And even if, with Wordsworth, you believed in the ability of poetry to poetize any conditions that modern technology might bring into being, you could question whether this result could be got through the Wordsworth aesthetic. Hence a century later, D. H. Lawrence, whose flower poems could have been models for Roethke, warns against a kind of *abstraction from the physical* that accompanies the progress of scientific materialism.

The doctrine infuses all of Lawrence's writings. But one can find it especially announced in his essay, "Men Must Work and Women as Well," reprinted in the Viking Portable. We think of statements like these: "Mr. Ford, being in his own way a genius, has realized that what the modern workman wants, just like the modern gentleman, is abstraction. The modern workman doesn't *want* to be interested in his job. He wants to be as little interested, as nearly perfectly mechanical, as possible." . . . The trend of our civilization is "towards a greater and greater abstraction from the physical, towards a further and further physical separateness between men and women, and between individual and individual." . . . Such displays even as "sitting in bathing suits all day on a beach" are "peculiarly non-physical, a flaunting of the body in its non-physical, merely optical aspect." . . . "He only *sees* his meal, he never *really* eats it. He drinks his beer by idea, he no longer tastes it." . . . "Under it all, as ever, as everywhere, vibrates the one great impulse of our civilization, physical recoil from every other being and from every form of physical existence." . . . "We can look on Soviet Russia as nothing but a logical state of society established in anti-physical insanity.—Physical and material are, of course, not the same; in fact, they are subtly opposite. The machine is absolutely material, and absolutely anti-physical—as even our fingers know. And the Soviet is established on the image of the machine, 'pure' materialism. The Soviet hates the real physical body far more deeply than it hates Capital." . . . "The only thing to do is to get your bodies back, men and women. A great part of society is irreparably lost: abstracted into non-physical, mechanical entities."

One may object to the particulars here; the *tendency* Lawrence discusses is clear enough. And though machinery (as viewed in psychoanalytic terms) may stand for the pudenda, and though the abstractions of technology and finance may even make for a compensatory overemphasizing of the sexual (Love Among the Machines), Lawrence was noting how the proliferation of mechanical means makes for a relative withdrawal, for a turn from intuitive immediacy to pragmatist meditation; hence his crusade against the intellect (and its "ideas").

As a novelist, Lawrence confronted this problem in all its contradictoriness. His crusade against the intellect was itself intellectual, even intellectualistic. Along with his cult of simplicity (which, going beyond Dante's infantile-maternal criterion and Wordsworth's rustic one, became a super-Rousseauistic vision of ideal savagery) there was his endless discussion of the issue. But though few modern novels contain a higher percentage of talk that might fall roughly under the heading of "ideas," (talk under the slogan, Down With Talk), in his verse he sought for images that *exemplified* the state of intuitive immediacy rather than expatiating on the problem of its loss. For whereas the novels dealt with people, the verse could treat of animals and inanimate beings that imagistically figured some generalized or idealized human motive (as with the heroic copulation of whales and elephants, or the social implications in the motions of a snapdragon). All told, he loquaciously celebrated the wisdom of silent things—for the yearning to see beyond the intellect terminates mystically in the yearning to regain a true state of "infancy," such immediacy of communication as would be possible only if man had never spoken at all (an aim often sought in sexual union, though both sexual barriers and the breaking of those barriers are preponderantly conditioned by the many "ideas of reason" that are the necessary result of language and of the social order made possible by language).

All told, then, we can see in Roethke's cult of "intuitive" language: a more strictly "infantile" variant of the Dantesque search for a "noble" vernacular; a somewhat suburban, horticulturist variant of Wordsworth's stress upon the universal nature of rusticity; and a close replica of Lawrence's distinction between the "physical" and the "abstract."

With "prowess in arms" (*Virtus*) he is not concerned. The long poems, still to be considered, are engrossed with problems of welfare (*Salus*), though of a kind attainable rather by persistent dreamlike yielding than by moralistic "guidance of the will." As for *Venus,* in Roethke's verse it would seem addressed most directly to a phase of adolescence. The infantile motif serves here, perhaps, like the persuasive gestures of sorrow or helplessness, as appeal to childless girls vaguely disposed toward nursing. The lost son's bid for a return to the womb may thus become transformed into a doting on the erotic imagery of the "sheath-wet" and its "slip-ooze." And in keeping, there is the vocabulary of flowers and fishes (used with connotations of love), and of primeval slime.

We have considered representative instances of Roethke's poetic manner. We have viewed his choice of terms from the standpoint of three motivational orders as described by Kant. And we noted three strategic moments in the theory of poetic selectivity (Dante on the infantile, Wordsworth on the rustic, Lawrence on the physical). Now let us ask what kind of selectivity is implicit in Roethke's flower images (with their variants of the infantile, rustic, and physical).

In particular, what is a greenhouse? What might we expect it to stand for? It is not sheer nature, like a jungle; nor even regulated nature, like a formal garden. It is not the starkly unnatural, like a factory. Nor is it in those intermediate realms of institutional lore, systematic thanatopses, or convenient views of death, we find among the relics of a natural history museum. Nor would it be like a metropolitan art gallery. It is like all these only in the sense that it is a museum experience, and so an aspect of our late civilization. But there is a peculiar balance of the natural and the artificial in a greenhouse. All about one, the lovely, straining beings, visibly drawing sustenance from ultimate, invisible powers—in a silent blare of vitality—yet as morbid as the caged animals of a zoo.

Even so, with Roethke the experience is not like going from exhibit to exhibit among botanic oddities and rarities. It is like merging there into the life-laden but sickly soil.

To get the quality of Roethke's affections, we should try thinking of "lubricity" as a "good" word, connoting the curative element in the primeval slime. Thus, with him, the image of the mire is usually felicitous, associated with protection and welcome, as in warm sheathlike forms. Only in moments of extremity does he swing to the opposite order of meanings, and think rather of the mire that can hold one a prisoner, sucking toward stagnation and death. Then, for a period of wretchedness, the poet is surprised into finding in this otherwise Edenic image, his own equivalent for Bunyan's slough of despond.

Flowers suggest analogous human motives quite as the figures of animals do in Aesop's fables (except that here they stand for relationships rather than for typical characters). The poet need but be as accurate as he can, in describing the flowers objectively; and while aiming at this, he comes upon corresponding human situations, as it were by redundancy. Here was a good vein of imagery to exploit, even as a conceit: that is, any poet shrewdly choosing a theme might hit upon hothouse imagery as generating principle for a group of poems. Yet in this poet's case there was a further incentive. His father had actually been a florist, in charge of a greenhouse. Hence, when utilizing the resources of this key image for new developments, Roethke could at the same time be drawing upon the most occult of early experiences. Deviously, elusively, under such conditions the amplifying of the theme could also be "regressive," and in-turning.

The duality, in the apparent simplicity, of his method probably leads back, as with the somewhat mystic *ars poetica* of so many contemporary poets, to the kind of order statuesquely expressed in Baudelaire's sonnet, *"Correspon-dances,"* on mankind's passage through nature as through "forests of symbols," while scents, sounds, and colors "make mutual rejoinder" like distant echoes that fuse "in deep and dusky unity."

In "Night Crow," Roethke states his equivalent of the pattern thus:

> When I saw that clumsy crow
> Flap from a wasted tree,
> A shape in the mind rose up:
> Over the gulfs of dream
> Flew a tremendous bird
> Further and further away
> Into a moonless black,
> Deep in the brain, far back.

One could take it as a particularized embodiment of a general principle, an anecdote of *one* image standing for the way of all such images, which are somehow felt twice, once positivistically, and once symbolically.

In this connection, even one misprint becomes meaningful. In "Weed Puller," he writes of flowers "tugging all day at perverse life." At least, that is the wording presumably intended. The line actually reads: "tugging at pre-verse life." In Roethke's case, this was indeed a "pre-verse" way of life. In the flowers, their hazards and quixotisms, he was trained to a symbolic vocabulary of subtle human relations and odd strivings, before he could have encountered the equivalent patterns of experience in exclusively human terms. As with those systems of pure mathematics which mathematicians sometimes develop without concern for utility, long before men in the practical realm begin asking themselves the kind of questions for which the inventor of the pure forms has already offered the answers; so, in the flower stories, the poet would be reverting to a time when he had noted these forms before he felt the need for them, except vaguely and "vatically."

The opposite way is depicted in a drawing (we falsely remembered it as a caricature) printed in *L'Illustration* and reproduced in Matthew Josephson's book on Emile Zola. It is entitled "Zola Studying Railroad Life on a Locomotive; Drawing Made on the Scene, During a Voyage Between Paris and Le Havre, When He Was Seeking the 'Living Documents' for his Novel, *La Bete Humaine*." Zola, standing, stiffly erect, between the cabin and the coal car, dressed in a semiformal attire that would suit a doctor or a lawyer of that time, is all set to make the trip that would supply him with certain required documentary observations for a "scientific" novel.

What, roughly, then, is the range of meaning in Roethke's flowers? In part, they are a kind of psychology, an emphatic vocabulary for expressing rudimentary motives felt, rightly or wrongly, to transcend particular periods of time. Often, in their characters as "the lovely diminutives," they are children in general, or girls specifically. When we are told in "The Waking" that "flowers jumped / Like small goats," there is a gracing of the bestial motive referred to as "the goat's mouth" in the "dance" of "The Long Alley," section three. The preconscious, the infantile, the regressive, the sexual—but is there not in them a further mystery, do they not also appeal as a pageantry, as "positions of pantomime," their natural beauty deriving added secular "sanctification" from the principle of hierarchy? For the thought of flowers, in their various conditions, with their many ways of root, sprout, and blossom, is like the contemplation of nobles, churchmen, commoners, peasants (a world of masks). In hothouse flowers, you confront, enigmatically, the representation of status. By their nature flowers contribute grace to social magic— hence, they are insignia, infused with a spirit of social ordination. In this respect they could be like Aesop's animals, though only incipiently so. For if their relation to the social mysteries were schematically recognized, we should emerge from the realm of intuitions (with their appropriate "aesthetic ideas") into such "ideas of reason" as a Pope might cultivate ("whatever is, is right" . . . "self-love, to urge, and reason, to restrain" . . . "force first made conquest, and that conquest, law" . . . "order is heaven's first law" . . . "that true self-love and social are the same"). A Roethke might well subscribe to some such doctrine, notably Pope's tributes to "honest Instinct"—but in terms whereby the assumptions would, within these rules of utterance, be themselves unutterable.

Other of the shorter poems should be mentioned, such as "My Papa's Waltz," which is dashing in its account of a boy whirled in a dance with his tipsy father; "Judge Not," a more formalistic statement than is characteristic. Some of the short pieces come close to standard magazine verse. "The Waking" risks a simple post-Wordsworthian account of pure joy. And "Pickle Belt," recounting "the itches / Of sixteen-year-old lust," while not of moment in itself, in its puns could be listed with the crow poem, if one were attempting to specify systematically just how many kinds of correspondence

Roethke's images draw upon. But mostly, here, we want to consider the four longer pieces: "The Lost Son," "The Long Alley," "A Field of Light," and "The Shape of the Fire."

Roethke himself has described them as "four experiences, each in a sense stages in a kind of struggle out of the slime; part of a slow spiritual progress, if you will; part of an effort to be born." At the risk of brashness, we would want to modify this description somewhat. The transformations seem like a struggle less to be born than to avoid being undone. Or put it thus: The dangers inherent in the regressive imagery seem to have received an impetus from without, that drove the poet still more forcefully in the same direction, dipping him in the river who loved water. His own lore thus threatened to turn against him. The enduring of such discomforts is a "birth" in the sense that, if the poet survives the ordeal, he is essentially stronger, and has to this extent *forged himself* an identity.

The four poems are, in general, an alternating of two motives: regression, and a nearly lost, but never quite relinquished, expectancy that leads to varying degrees of fulfillment. In "Flight," the first section of "The Lost Son," the problem is stated impressionistically, beginning with the mention of death ("concretized," of course, not in the name of "death," which would be at the farthest an abstraction, at the nearest an abstraction personified, but circumstantially: "At Woodlawn I heard the dead cry"). When considering the possible thesaurus of flowers, we were struck by the fact that, in the greenhouse poems, there was no overt reference to the use of flowers for the sickroom and as funeral wreaths. Deathy connotations are implicitly there, at the very start, in the account of the Cuttings, which are dying even as they strain heroically to live. And there is the refuse of "Flower Dump." But of flowers as standing for the final term of human life, we recall no mention. Roethke has said that he conceives of the greenhouse as symbol for "a womb, a heaven-on-earth." And the thought of its vital internality, in this sense, seems to have obliterated any conscious concern with the uses to which the products of the florist's trade are put. In any case his present poem, dealing with a lyric "I" in serious danger, fittingly begins in the sign of death.

The opening stanza, however, contains not merely the theme of deathlike stagnation. There is also, vaguely, talk of moving on:

>Snail, snail, glister me forward,
>Bird, soft-sigh me home.

In the society of *this* poet's lowly organisms, there is a curative element, incipiently. And throughout the opening section, with its images of rot and stoppage, there is likewise a watching and waiting. Even a rhetorical *question* is, after all, subtly, in form a *quest*. Hence the call for a sign ("Out of what

door do I go, / Where and to whom?"), though it leads but to veiled oracular
answers ("Dark hollows said, lee to the wind, / The moon said, back of an
eel," etc.), transforms this opening section ("The Flight") into a hunt, however perplexed. Thus the stanza that begins "Running lightly over spongy
ground," is followed by one that begins, "Hunting along the river." The
section ends on a riddle, in terms contradictory and symbolic, as befits such
utterance. The connotations are Sphinxlike, oracular; the descriptions seem
to touch upon an ultimate wordless secret. What is the answer? Put all the
disjunct details together, and, for our purposes, we need but note that the
object of the quest is lubricitous (in the mode of furtive felicity). End of
Section One.

Section Two: The Pit—nine lines, in very subdued tonality, about roots—in
general an amplification of the statement that the poet's search is radical. We
cite the passage entire, since it is a splendid text for revealing the ingenuity of
Roethke as Rhetorician:

> Where do the roots go?
>   Look down under the leaves.
> Who put the moss there?
>   These stones have been here too long.
> Who stunned the dirt into noise?
>   Ask the mole, he knows.
> I feel the slime of a wet nest.
>   Beware Mother Mildew.
> Nibble again, fish nerves.

Considered as topics ("places" in the traditional rhetorical sense), the
stanza could be reduced to a set of images that variously repeat the idea of
the deep-down, the submerged, the underground. Roots . . . "under the
leaves" . . . stones long buried beneath moss . . . the sound of moles burrowing . . . these are details that variously repeat the same theme in the first six
lines. The last three, while similar in quality (the dank, hidden, submerged,
within), add a further development: the hint of incipience, ambiguously
present in lines seven and eight ("I feel" and "Beware"), comes clear in line
nine: "Nibble again, fish nerves."

For the moment confining ourselves to the first six: note how this series of
lyric images is dramatized. Surprisingly, much is done by a purely Grammatical resource. Thus, the underlying assertion of the first couplet (this mood is
like roots, like under-the-leaves) is transformed into a kind of "cosmic"
dialogue, split into an interchange between two voices. The next restatement
(it is like moss-covered stones) is broken into the same Q-A pattern, but this
time the answer is slightly evasive, though still in the indicative ("These

stones have been here too long," a "vatic" way of suggesting that the mood is like stones sunken, and covered heavily). The third couplet (it is like the sound of moles burrowing) is introduced by a slightly longer and more complex form of question. (The first was where-roots-go, the second who-put-moss-there, and the third is who-stunned-dirt-into-noise, a subtly growing series). Also the answer is varied by a shift into the imperative ("ask the mole").

All this questioning and answering has been as if from voices in the air, or in the nature of things. But the turn in the last three lines is announced by a shift to the lyric "I" as subject. The image of mildew is made not only personal, but "essential," by being named as "Mother Mildew." The indicative in line seven ("I feel") shifts to imperatives in lines eight and nine ("Beware" and "Nibble"); but whereas in the first of these imperatives the topic (mildew) appears as object of the command, in the second the topic ("fish nerves") is given as subject.

Thus, though the stanza is but a series of restatements, it has considerable variety despite the brevity of the lines and despite the fact that each sentence ends exactly at the end of a line. And the Grammatical shifts, by dramatizing the sequence of topics, keep one from noting that the stanza is in essence but a series of similarly disposed images (symbolizing what Roethke, in a critical reference, has called "obsessions").

As for the closing line, the more one knows of the fish image in Roethke's verse, the more clearly one will feel the quality of incipience in the nibbling of "fish nerves."

The third section, "The Gibber," might (within the conditions of a lyric) be said to culminate in the *act* that corresponds to the attitude implicit in the opening scene. It is sexual, but reflexively so: the poet is disastrously alone. Listening, "by the cave's door," the poet hears an old call ("Dogs of the groin / Barked and howled," and sinister things, in the mood of a Walpurgisnacht, call for his yielding in a kind of death). Against a freezing fear, there is a desperate cry for infantile warmth. "I'm cold. I'm cold all over. Rub me in father and mother." The reflexive motif is most direct, perhaps, in the lines: "As my own tongue kissed / My lips awake." The next lines (Roethke has called them a kind of Elizabethan "rant") culminate in a shrilly plaintive inventory of the hero's plight:

> All the windows are burning! What's left of my life?
> I want the old rage, the lash of primordial milk!
> Goodbye, goodbye, old stones, the time-order is going,
> I have married my hands to perpetual agitation,
> I run, I run to the whistle of money,

the lamentation being summed up, by a break in a different rhythm:

> Money money money
> Water water water

Roethke's Vegetal Radicalism is not the place one would ordinarily look for comments on the economic motive. Yet you can take it as a law that, in our culture, at a moment of extreme mental anguish, if the sufferer is accurate there will be an accounting of money, too. It will be at least implicit, in the offing—hence with professional utterers it should be explicit. So, the agitation comes to a head in the juxtaposing of two liquidities, two potencies, one out of society, the other universal, out of nature. (And in the typical dichotomy of aestheticism, where the aesthetic and the practical are treated as in diametrical opposition to each other, does not this alignment encourage us to treat art and the rational as antitheses? For if money is equated with the practical and the rational, then by the dialectics of the case art is on the side of an "irrational," nonmonetary Nature.)

After a brief rush of scenic details (cool grass, a bird that may have gone away, a swaying stalk, the shadow of a worm, undirected clouds—all developed by the Grammatico-Rhetorical method we noted in "The Pit") the section ends on a world of white flashes, which the poet finally characterizes as of the essence of cinder "falling through a dark swirl."

Into the funnel: down the drain. The dream-death. Though the second section was *entitled* "The Pit," here actually is the poem's abysmal moment, after which there must be a turning.

Hence, Section Four, "The Return." Recovery in terms of the "father principle." Memory of a greenhouse experience: out of night, the coming of dawn, and the father. After the description of the dark, with the roses likened to bloody clinkers in a furnace (an excellently right transition from the ashes theme at the close of the previous section to the topic of steam knocking in the steam pipes as a heralding of the advent), the movement proceeds thus (note that the theme of white is also kept and appropriately transformed):

> Once I stayed all night.
> The light in the morning came up slowly over the white
> Snow.
> There were many kinds of cool
> Air.
> Then came steam.
>
> Pipe-knock.
>
> Scurry of warm over small plants.
> Ordnung! ordnung!
> Papa is coming!

We happen to have seen a comment which Roethke wrote on this passage, and we cite it for its great use in revealing his methods:

> Buried in the text are many little ambiguities that are not always absolutely necessary to know. For instance, the "pipe-knock." With the coming of steam, the pipes begin knocking violently, in a greenhouse. But "Papa," or the florist, often would knock his own pipe (a pipe for smoking) on the sides of the benches, or the pipes . . . Then, with the coming of steam (and "papa"—the papa on earth and heaven being blended, of course) there is the sense of motion in the greenhouse—my symbol for the whole of life, a womb, a heaven-on-earth.

Recalling De Quincey's comments on the knocking at the gate after the murder scene in Macbeth, and recalling that we have just been through a "suicide" scene, might we not also include, among the connotations of this sound, the knock of conscience? Particularly in that the return to the paternally (or "superegoistically") rational is announced in terms of an admonition (*Ordnung! ordnung!*)—and we should note, on the side, as a possible motivating factor in Roethke's avoidance of ideational abstraction, that this German word for order is one of his few such expressions, though here it has practically the force of an imperative verb, as "sweetness," in another context, was not in function an abstract noun but rather a *name,* an epithet of personal endearment. (Roethke has said that he had in mind the father's Prussian love of discipline, as sublimated into the care of flowers; and he wanted to suggest that the child, as a kind of sleepy sentry, "jumped to attention at the approach.")

The final section (sans title) amplifies the subject of illumination (that we have followed from darkness, through "white flashes," to dawn). But its opening suggests its unfinishedness (as with a corresponding midstage in Eliot's *Four Quartets*):

> It was beginning winter,
> An in-between time . . .

And after talk of light (and reflexively, "light within light") the poem ends on his variant of religious patience and vigil, as applied to the problem of superegoistic rationality:

> A lively understandable spirit
> Once entertained you.
> It will come again.
> Be still.
> Wait.

Again the funnel, in the narrowing-down of the lines. But not, this time, the funnel of darkness that had marked the end of Section Three. There has been a coming of light after darkness, a coming of warmth after cold, a coming of steam after powerlessness, a coming of the father and of his superegoistic knock—and now at the last a fuller coming is promised. And within the rules of this idiom, "understandable" is a perfect discovery. It is perhaps the only "intellectualistic" word (the only word for "rational") that would not have jarred in this context.

All four of the long poems follow this same general pattern. Thus, "The Long Alley" begins with a sluggish near-stagnant current (from sources outside the poem we have learned that this brooding, regressive stream is "by the edge of the city"). Direction is slight but it is there:

> A river glides out of the grass. A river or serpent.
> A fish floats belly upward,
> Sliding through the white current,
> Slowing turning,
> Slowly.

But the way out is roundabout, a way in. Next there are apostrophes to an absent "kitten-limp sister," a "milk-nose," a "sweetness I cannot touch," as our hero complains that he needs "a loan of the quick." And the stanza ends narcissistically. In the third section, after a plea again reflexively addressed ("Have mercy, gristle") there is an agitated "dance," a simulated *argutatio lecti* (Catullus 6, 11) conveyed somewhat impressionistically, symbolically, enigmatically. After this "close knock," again struggling toward warmth ("Sweet Jesus, make me sweat," a musically felicitous cry, in that the last word is an umlaut modification of the first: sw——t sw——t), there is a somewhat idealistic vision, a gentle name-calling, in which girls ("tenderest") are "littlest flowers" with "fish-ways," while the talk of light ("drowsing in soft light" . . . "Light airs! A piece of angels!") prepares for the closing stanza with its talk of warmth. The progress of the sections might be indicated by these summarizing lines: (1) "My gates are all caves"; (2) "Return the gaze of a pond" (an ingenious inversion of the Narcissus image); (3) "I'm happy with my paws"; (4) "The tendrils have me"; (5) "I'll take the fire."

The shortest of the four long poems, "A Field of Light," begins similarly with "dead water" and evolves into a celebrating of "the lovely diminutives," while the poet walked "through the light air" and "moved with the morning." The mood is most succinctly conveyed, perhaps, in the line: "Some morning thing came, beating its wings." The poem is in three stages: (1) The "dead water," but almost pleasantly, a "watery drowse"; (2) the question-like and questionable act ("Alone, I kissed the skin of a stone; marrow-soft, danced in the sand"); (3) Exhilarated sense of promise.

However, despite the alleviation here, in the final poem, "The Shape of the Fire," the entire course is traveled again. Indeed, if we can accept the ingenious suggestion of one commentator (Mr. Bill Brown, a student in a poetry class of Roethke's), the line "An old scow bumps over black rocks" is about as regressive as human memory could be. It suggests to him "the heart-beat of the mother," as the fetus might hear it dully while asleep in the amniotic fluid, the ultimately regressive baptismal water. (Such reminiscence from prenatal experience would be a purely naturalistic equivalent for the "clouds of glory" that Wordsworth Platonically saw the infant memory "trailing" from its "immortal" past.) In any case, at the very least, the line suggests the state of near-stagnation, a stream so low that a boat of even the shallowest draught scrapes bottom. And after a reflexive section ("My meat eats me," while before this there was but half a being, "only one shoe" and "a two-legged dog"), and a section on vigil ("The wasp waits"), and one to announce awakening promise ("Love, love sang toward," a pleasantly impressionistic idyll of early happiness at the age when childhood was merging into puberty), now the boat can again figure, but transfigured, to assert direction:

> To stare into the after-light, the glitter left on the lake's surface,
> When the sun has fallen behind a wooded island;
> To follow the drops sliding from a lifted oar,
> Held up, while the rower breathes, and the small boat drifts quietly
>   shoreward;
> To know that light falls and fills, often without our knowing,
> As an opaque vase fills to the brim from a quick pouring,
> Fills and trembles at the edge yet does not flow over,
> Still holding and feeding the stem of the contained flower.

Thus, at the end, the cut flower with which the book began. And though the image of the gliding boat (as contrasted with the bottom-scraping one) has moved us from stagnation to felicity (here is a resting on one's oars, whereas Shelley's enrapt boats proceed even without a rower), note that the position of the poet in the advancing craft is backward-looking. Still, there is testimony to a delight in seeing, in contrast with Baudelaire's poem on Don Juan crossing the Styx, similarly looking back: Charon steered the craft among the shades in torment,

> Mais le calme héros, courbé sur sa rapière,
> Regardait le sillage et ne daignait rien voir.

As for all the possible connotations in light, as used in the final illumination of the Roethke poem, spying, we may recall that the last line of the second section was: "Renew the light, lewd whisper."

All told, to analyze the longer poems[2] one should get the general "idea" (or better, mood or *attitude*) of each stanza, then note the succession of images that actualize and amplify it. Insofar as these images are of visible, tangible things, each will be given its verb, so that it have sufficient incidental vividness. But though, in a general way, these verbs will be, either directly or remotely, of the sort that usually goes with the thing (as were dogs to bark, or pigs to grunt), often there may be no verb that, within the conditions of the poem, the noun objectively requires.

For instance, at the beginning of "The Shape of the Fire," there is a line "A cracked pod calls." As an image, the cracked pod belongs here. It is dead, yet there is possibility of a new life in it. Hence, topically, the line might have read simply "A cracked pod." Similarly, there is the line, "Water recedes to the crying of spiders." If spiders stand in general for the loathsome, the line might be translated formalistically: "The principle of fertility is overcome by the principle of fear." However, though pods may rattle, and spiders may weave or bite or trap flies, pods don't call and spiders don't cry.[3]

In considering this problem most pedestrianly, we believe we discovered another Rhetorical device which Roethke has used quite effectively. That is, whenever there is no specific verb required, Roethke resorts to some word in the general category of *communication*. Thus, though "shale loosens" and "a low mouth laps water," a cracked pod calls, spiders and snakes cry, weeds whine, dark hollows, the moon and salt say, inanimate things answer and question and listen or are listened to. To suggest that one thing is of the same essence as another, the poet can speak of their kissing, that is, being in intimate communion (a device that has unintended lewd overtones at one point where the poet, to suggest that he is of the essence of refuse, says, "Kiss

---

[2]Incidentally, there are records of "The Long Alley" and "The Shape of the Fire," as read by the author (Poetry Room, Harvard College Library: *The Harvard Vocarium Records*). Some of the tonalities are strikingly like those in the record of Joyce's readings from *Anna Livia Plurabelle*.

[3]Though our "formalistic" version here would be acceptable as a "first rough approximate" of the meaning, there are further possibilities in the offing. Psychoanalytically, insects are said to figure often in dreams as surrogates for children. And in an earlier version of the lyric, "Judge Not," a reference to "the unborn, starving in wombs, curling" had used the same image: the fetuses were described as curling "like dried spiders." The line, "Water recedes to the crying of spiders" might thus, if trailed far enough, bring us into the region of the "birth trauma," as figuring an infant cry at separation from the placental bath. And since the line is immediately followed by "An old scow bumps over black rocks," the child as crying spider could fit well with the already cited interpretation of this second line. (The matter of the order would not be all-important. In the elliptical style, the stages of a development may readily become reordered.)

me, ashes," a hard line to read aloud without disaster, unless one pauses long on the comma). The topic is clouds? Not clouds that billow or blow, but that would just *be*? The line becomes: "What do the clouds *say*?"

There are possible objections to be raised against this sort of standard poetic personifying, which amounts to putting a communicative verb where the copula is normally required, or perhaps one could have no verb at all. But it does help to suggest a world of natural objects in vigorous communication with one another. The very least these poetic entities do is resort to "mystic participation." The poet's scene constitutes a society of animals and things. To walk through his idealized Nature is to be surrounded by figures variously greeting, beckoning, calling, answering one another, or with little groups here and there in confidential huddles, or strangers by the wayside waiting to pose Sphinxlike questions or to propound obscure but truth-laden riddles. One thus lives as though ever on the edge of an Ultimate Revelation. And as a clear instance of the method as a device for dramatization, consider a passage in "The Lost Son," which, topically considered, amounts to saying, "This is like dying in a weedy meadow, among snakes, cows, and briars," but is transformed by communicative verbs thus:

> The weeds whined,
> The snakes cried,
> The cows and briars
> Said to me: Die.

Somewhat incongruously, we have expressed the underlying statement in terms of simile. Yet similes are very rare in Roethke. The word "like" appears, unless we counted wrong, but three times in the four long poems; "as," used as a synonym for "like," occurs not much oftener. Indeed, one way to glimpse the basic method used here is to think, first, of simile, next of metaphor, and then (extrapolating) imagine advancing to a further step. Thus, one might say, in simile, "The toothache is like a raging storm," or metaphorically, "The raging tooth." Or "beyond" that, one might go elliptically, without logical connectives, from talk of toothache to talk of ships storm-tossed at sea. And there one would confront the kind of *ars poetica* in which Roethke is working.

The method may be further extended by the use of a word in accordance with pure pun-logic. Thus, if in "reach" you hear "rich," you may say either "reach me" or "rich me" for the reach that enriches. ("Rich me cherries a fondling's kiss.")

Much of this verse is highly auditory, leaving implicit the kind of tonal transformations that Hopkins makes explicit. And often the ellipses, by weakening strictly logical attention, induce the hearer to flutter on the edge of associations not surely present, but evanescently there, and acutely evocative (to those who receive poetry through ear rather than eye).

Surely in a poem still to be considered, "God, give me a near" is a barely audible extending of the sense in "God, give me an ear" (here the tonal effect is surest if approached through visual reading); and in the same poem, "tree" and "time" have been "irresponsibly" transposed, with suggestive effects, thus: "Once upon a tree / I came across a time." "The ear's not here / Beneath the hair" (in the opening stanza of Section Two, "The Shape of the Fire") is tonal improvising, which leads one vaguely to think of the ear as surrogate for a different order of receptacle. And in the lines immediately following ("When I took off my clothes / To find a nose, / There was only one / For the waltz of To, / The pinch of Where"), besides "to" in the sense of "toward," there are suggestions of "two" (here present in its denial, but the meaning most prominent to an auditor who does not have the page before him), while there are also connotations of "toe" as in toe dance (which in turn stirs up a belfry of bat-thoughts when we consider the narcissistic nature of this particular "toe dance," recall similarly the "last waltz with an old itch" in "The Long Alley," and then flutter vaguely in the direction of the infantile "polymorphous perverse" as we think of the briskly and brilliantly conveyed corybantics in the brief lyric, "My Papa's Waltz," the account of a child snatched up and whirled riotously in a dance by his tipsy father). And since "t" is but an unvoiced "d," we believe that, on the purely tonal level, "God" may be heard in "gate." In any case, in "The Long Alley" there are but three lines elliptically separating "this smoke's from the glory of God" and "My gates are all caves."

Though Roethke's lines often suggest spontaneous simplicity, and though the author has doubtless so cultivated this effect that many lines do originally present themselves in such a form, on occasion the simplicity may be got only after considerable revision. Thus, in an early version of "The Shape of the Fire," there had been a passage:

> The wind sharpened itself on a rock. It began raining.
> Finally, having exhausted the possibilities of common sense,
> I composed the following: . . .

"It began raining" was later changed to "Rain began falling." An earlier version had been, "It rains offal," but this, though more accurate, had to be abandoned presumably because of its closeness to "It rains awful." Eventually the reference to rain was dropped completely—for if the essence of this rain (its quality as motive) could not be specified, the reference was perhaps better omitted. The second and third lines were changed to: "Finally, to interrupt that particular monotony, / I intoned the following." Both versions thus sounded self-conscious and formalistic, whereas the final version is naïvely vatic:

> The wind sharpened itself on a rock;
> A voice sang: . . .

The "I" of the versifier at work has been replaced by a cosmically communicating "voice."

Stanley Kunitz, reviewing *The Lost Son and Other Poems* in POETRY, justly observes:

> The sub-human is given tongue; and what the tongue proclaims is the agony of coming alive, the painful miracle of growth. Here is a poetry immersed in the destructive element. It would seem that Roethke has reached the limits of exploration in this direction, that the next step beyond must be either silence or gibberish. Yet the daemon is with him, and there is no telling what surprises await us.

Reverting, in this connection, to our talk of intuitions, concepts, and ideas, and recalling the contrast between the vocabulary of these poems and that of Eliot's *Quartets,* we might put the matter thus, in seeking to characterize Roethke's "way":

There is a realm of motives local to the body, and there is a possible ultimate realm, of motives derived from the Ground of All Existence, whatever that may be. In between, there are the motives of man-made institutions, motives located generally in the terminologies of technology, business, politics, social institutions, and the like. Here are many titular words, abstractions, "ideas of reason," to name the realm midway between the pains, pleasures, appetites of the individual body and the Universal Ground.

Since the body emerges out of nature, its language seems closer to the ultimate realm of motives than do the abstractions of politics. However, the pleasures, pains, fears, and appetites of the body are all, in subtle ways, molded by the forms of the political realm; hence what we take as "nature" is largely a social pageant in disguise. But the vocabulary of traffic regulation is alien to the "noble" speech of childhood emerging from infancy. (Parker Tyler, so often excellent in his insights, convincingly points to the "aristocratic" element in Charlie Chaplin's child motif. And Nietzsche, in his *Genealogy of Morals,* might better be talking of a child when he cites, as his example of the aristocrat, the person whose resentment "fulfils and exhausts itself in an immediate reaction, and consequently instills no *venom,*" while this resentment "never manifests itself at all in countless instances," since "strong natures" cannot "take seriously for any length of time their enemies, their disasters, their *misdeeds*," and forgive insult simply because they forget it.)

In any case, as tested by the simplicity of the "natural" vocabulary, the forensic sub-Ciceronian speech is "barbaric." And though we may, by round-about devices, disclose how politics, through the medium of family relations, affects the child's experiences at the very start of life, the *ideas* are certainly not there—hence the "purest" vocabulary is that of the emotionally tinged perceptions (the "intuitions of sensibility").

But how much of human motivation is the poet to encompass in his work? Or, next, how much is he to encompass *directly, explicitly,* and how much by *implication,* by resonances derived from sympathetic vibrations in the offing? There comes a time, in life itself, when one flatly confronts the realm of social hierarchy (in the scramble to get or to retain or to rewardingly use money, position, prestige). Will one, then, if a poet, seek to discuss these motives just as flatly in his poetic medium? Or will he conceive of poetry by antithesis (as so many of our poets, now teaching poetry, place it in direct antithesis to their means of livelihood, hence contending that the "aesthetic" is precisely what the "didactic" is not)?

It is not for critics, in their task of characterization, to legislate for the poet here. It is enough to note that there are several methods of confronting the problem, and that Roethke's work has thoroughly and imaginatively ex-emplified one of them. He meets, in his way, the problem which Eliot met in another by expanding his poetry to encompass theological doctrine, and thereby including a terminology which, within the Roethke rules, would be ungainly (unless used ironically—and children don't take to irony). Eliot added winds of doctrine. Roethke "regressed" as thoroughly as he could, even at considerable risk, toward a language of sheer "intuition."

However, our use of the Kantian pattern will deceive us, if we conclude that such intuitions really do remain on the level of "sensation." For not only do they require the "concept" (as a name that clamps intellectual unity upon a given manifold of sensations); they also involve motives beyond both sense and understanding: we go from intuitions of a sensory sort to intuitions of a *symbolic* sort (as with the motives of the "unconscious" which make variously for fusion, confusion, diffusion). In scholastic usage, by "intuition" was meant the recognition that something is as it is. The term was not restricted merely to sense perception. Not only would color, sound, or odor be an intuition; but there would be intuition in the recognition that two and two make four, or that a complex problem is solvable in a certain way, or that a science rests on such and such principles. Applied to modern poetizing, the word might also be used to name a situation when the poet chooses an expression because it "feels right," though he might not be able to account for the choice rationalistically. The judgment would rely on such motives as are, under favorable circumstances, disclosable psychoanalytically, or may be idealistic counterparts of hierarchic motives (a "beauty" involving *social* distinction between the noble and the vulgar, mastery and enslavement, loveliness and crassness); and there may also be included here responses to the incentives of pun-logic.

Thus, if in one context the image of a flower can stand for girlhood in general, and if in other contexts a fish can have similar connotations, in still other contexts flower and fish can be elliptically merged (for reasons beyond the fact that the one can be plucked and the other caught), producing what we might call a "symbolic intuition" atop the purely sensory kind. Or we might consider such idealistic mergers a symbolist variant of the "aesthetic idea" (as distinguished from "ideas of reason" in the more strictly rationalist sense). They are "fusions" if you like them, "confusions" if you don't, and "diffusions" when their disjunction outweighs their conjunction. And they are a resource of all our "objectivist" poets who use "positive" terms to elicit effects beyond the positive. Particularly we are in a purely idealistic (rather than positivistic) order of intuitions when we extend the motifs, going from fish to water and from flower to warmth or light, and hence from water to motions that are like pouring, or from flowers to motions that are like swaying (so that a sudden influx of birds might be a symbol descending through the fish-water-girl line, or a swaying tree might descend through the flower-warmth-girl side of the family, the two branches being reunited if the tree is swaying over water, after talk of a swaying fish).

This is the liquescent realm in which Roethke operates. But by eschewing the "rationality" of doctrine (a "parental principle" which one may situate in identification with father governments or mother churches, or with lesser brotherhoods themselves authoritatively endowed), the poet is forced into a "regressive" search for the "superego," as with talk of being "rubbed" . . . "in father and mother." Eliot could thus "rub" himself in dogma, borrowed from the intellectual matrix of the church. But Roethke, while avidly in search of an essential parenthood, would glumly reject incorporation in any cause or movement or institution as the new parent (at least so far as his poetic idiom is concerned). Hence his search for essential motives has driven him back into the quandaries of adolescence, childhood, even infancy. Also, as we have noted elsewhere, the search for essence being a search for "first principles," there is a purely technical inducement to look for definition in terms of one's absolute past; for a *narrative* vocabulary, such as is natural to poetry, invites one to state essence (priority) in *temporal* terms, as with Platonist "reminiscence"—an enterprise that leads readily to "mystic" intuitions of womb heaven and primeval slime.

The battle is a fundamental one. Hence the poems give the feeling of being "eschatological," concerned with first and last things. Where their positivism dissolves into mysticism, they suggest a kind of phallic pantheism. And the constant reverberations about the edges of the images give the excitement of being on the edge of Revelation (or suggest a state of vigil, the hope of getting the girl, of getting a medal, of seeing God). There is the pious awaiting of the good message—and there is response to "the spoor that spurs."

Later poems repeat the regressive imagery without the abysmal anguish. Thus, in "Praise to the End!" our hero, expanding in a mood of self-play ("What a bone-ache I have"... "Prickle-me"... "I'm a duke of eels"... "I'll feed the ghost alone. / Father, forgive my hands"... "The river's alone with its water. / All risings / Fall") follows with snatches of wonder-struck childhood reminiscence mixed with amative promise:

> Mips and ma the mooly moo,
> The like of him is biting who,
> A cow's a care and who's a coo?—
> What footie does is final.

He ends by asking to be laved in "ultimate waters," surrounded by "birds and small fish." And a line in the opening ("stagnation") section of "The Long Alley" ("My gates are all caves") is now echoed in an altered form happy enough to serve in the upsurge of the final stanza: "My ghosts are all gay." Along with the nursery jingles, some lines are allowed to remain wholly "unsimplified":

> It's necessary, among the flies and bananas, to keep a constant vigil,
> For the attacks of false humility take sudden turns for the worse.

"Where Knock Is Open Wide" is a placid depiction of childhood sensibility and reverie, in a post-Blake, post-Crazy Jane medium close to the quality of Mother Goose, with many "oracular" lines, in Sibylline ways near to the sound of nonsense. The poem progresses thus: thoughts about a kitten (it can "bite with its feet"); lullaby ("sing me a sleep-song, please"); dreams; the parents; an uncle that died ("he's gone for always"... "they'll jump on his belly"); singing in infancy; an owl in the distance; "happy hands"; a walk by the river; a fish dying in the bottom of a boat ("he's trying to talk"); the watering of roses ("the stems said, Thank you"). But "That was before. I fell! I fell!" Thereafter, talk of "nowhere," "cold," and "wind," the death of birds, followed by a paradigm of courtship: "I'll be a bite. You be a wink. / Sing the snake to sleep." And finally: "God's somewhere else. / ... Maybe God has a house. / But not here."

The title, though borrowed, is extremely apt in suggesting the kind of motivation which Roethke would reconstruct for us. Recall, for instance, Coleridge's distinction between "motive" and "impulse" (a distinction later revised somewhat in his theological writings, but clearly maintained while his reasoning was in accordance with the aesthetic of "The Eolian Harp"). By "motives" Coleridge meant such springs of action as derive from "interests." Bentham's utilitarian grounds of conduct, for instance, would be "motives." But "impulse" is spontaneous, a response free of all *arrière-pensée*, all ulterior purpose. Here, the answer would be as prompt as the call, would be one with the call. In the world of the adult Scramble, such a state of affairs would indeed be a happy hunting ground for hunters—and whoever is in fear of loss must, at the startling knock on the door, hasten to hide the treasure before opening. However, in the theme of childhood reverie, as ideally reconstructed, the poet can contemplate an Edenic realm of pure impulsiveness.

Yet perhaps it is not wholly without *arrière-pensée*. For is the motivation here as sheerly "regressive" as it may at first seem? Is not this recondite "baby-talk" also, considered as rhetoric, one mode of lover-appeal? And considering mention of the wink and the bite in connection with talk of the fall, might we not also discern an outcropping of double meanings, whether intended or not, in reference to a "mooly man" who "had a rubber hat" and "kept it in a can"? The cloaking of the utterance in such apparent simplicity may not prevent conception of an adult sort here, particularly as the lines are followed immediately by talk of "papa-seed."

What next? The placid evocation of childhood might well be carried further (the period of anguished evocations has presumably been safely weathered). Further readings in mystic literature could lead to more developments in the materializing of "spirit" (as in "The Visitant"). But a turn toward the doctrinaire and didactic (the socially "global" as against the sensitively "ultimate") would seem possible only if all this poet's past methods and skills were abandoned.

There is another already indicated possibility, however, which we might define by making a distinction between "personification" and "personalization." And we might get at the matter thus:

Though Roethke has dealt always with very concrete things, there is a sense in which these very concretions are abstractions. Notably, the theme of sex in his poems has been highly generalized, however intensely felt. His outcries concern erotic and autoerotic motives generically, the Feminine as attribute of a class. Or, though he may have had an individual in mind at the moment, there is no personal particularization in his epithets, so far as the reader is concerned. He courts Woman, as a Commoner might court The Nobility (though of course he has his own "pastoral" variants of the courtly, or coy, relation).

But because his imagism merges into symbolism, his flowers and fishes become Woman in the Absolute. That is what we would mean by "personification."

By "personalization," on the other hand, we would mean the greater *individualizing* of human relations. (Not total individualizing, however, for Aristotle reminds us that poetry is closer than history to philosophy, and philosophy seeks high generalization, whereas historical eras, in their exact combination of events, are unique.) In any case, we have seen one recent poem in which Roethke has attempted "personalization" as we have here defined it: "Elegy for Jane (My student, thrown by a horse)." Though not so finished a poem as "The Visitant," it conveys a tribute of heartfelt poignancy, in a pious gallantry of the quick confronting the dead, and ending:

> If only I could nudge you from this sleep,
> My maimed darling, my skittery pigeon.
> Over this damp grave I speak the words of my love:
> I, with no rights in this matter,
> Neither father nor lover.

Perhaps more such portraits, on less solemn occasions, will be the Next Phase? Meanwhile, our salute to the very relevant work that Roethke has already accomplished, both for what it is in itself, and for its typicality, its interest as representative of one poetic way which many others are also taking, with varying thoroughness.[4]

---

[4] I had long planned to revise this article (which was published sixteen years ago). I had hoped to bring it up to date by discussing Theodore Roethke's later work, and to make some of my original observations more precise. But I have finally decided to leave the piece just as it was, along with its several fumblings. For I cannot better contrive to suggest the rare, enticing danger of Roethke's verse, as I felt it then, and still do. Looking back now, in the light of his body's sudden yielding into death, can we not see the end vatically foretold when the connotations of vibrancy in his image of the fish become transformed into connotations of putrescence? And, if the heart stops at a moment of total mystic drought, do we not find that moment ambiguously and even jauntily introduced, through the delightful lines on "The Sloth"? With both this essay and the one following, my memory of voice and manner is imperious in ways that I have not at all been able to indicate.

Jerome Mazzaro

Theodore Roethke and the Failures of Language

A reader of Theodore Roethke's *Open House* (1941) soon comes upon a problem that bothered Roethke throughout most of his career—the problem of voice. Even as late as 1959, he felt the need, in "How to Write Like Somebody Else," to respond to charges by critics that after *Praise to the End!* (1951) his poetry became too imitative of others and himself. He explains that *Open House* had appropriated tones from Elinor Wylie, theories from W. H. Auden, and cadences from Léonie Adams in what he describes as a metaphoric Adams-Roethke literary "affair": "I loved her so much, her poetry, that I just *had* to become, for a brief moment, a part of her world. . . . I *had* to create something that would honor her in her own terms." He adds in his defense, "I didn't cabbage those effects in cold blood." He opposes this affectionate theft to his later "conscious imitation" of established writers. Here, he asserts, the very fact the poet "has the support of a tradition, of an older writer, will enable him to be more himself—or more than himself." In between, when he was reordering in verse memories of Saginaw and the greenhouse world of his childhood, he confessed in an "Open Letter" to John Ciardi (1950) that he served as an "instrument" for the poems much as W. B. Yeats claimed his wife had in the writing of *A Vision* (1917). As quoted by Allan Seager in *The Glass House* (1968), Jim Jackson, who taught with Roethke at Bennington when Roethke began the poems, supports such a view: "*Lost Son* was written in huge swatches. With run-on chants, dirges coming forth pell-mell. Sense of continuity uppermost at all times—even though particular poems in *Lost Son* were later detached and presented as individual poems."

This role of poet-as-instrument coincides with the notion of style Goethe proposes in "Simple Imitation of Nature, Manner, Style" (1789). For Goethe, style "rests on the deepest fundamental ground of knowledge, on the essence of things, insofar as it is granted us to know this in visible and tangible forms." Roethke derives the role from Rainer Maria Rilke, who in *The Note-books of Malte Laurids Brigge* (1910) mentions the writer's need to be able to think back with more than memories. Like William Wordsworth's "emotions recollected in tranquility," "one must be able to forget them and have vast patience until . . . they become blood within us, and glances and

From *Modern Poetry Studies*, 1, 2 (July 1970), 73-96. Reprinted by permission of the author and *Modern Poetry Studies*.

gestures [;] . . . then first it can happen that in a rare hour the first word of a verse may arise and come forth." In "On 'Identity' " (1963), Roethke uses Rilke as a model for heightening one's awareness of the universe: "To look at a thing so long that you are part of it and it is a part of you—Rilke gazing at his tiger ["Der Panther"?] for eight hours, for instance." Reversing his early aversion to tradition, Roethke extends this heightening to the dead as well as to the living: "If the dead can come to our aid in our quest for identity, so can the living—and I mean all living things, including the sub-human." The process, Seager reports Judith Bailey as telling him, was extended also to inanimate objects: "She says she believes that Ted actually abused his mind by concentrating on single objects for so long at a time, and she says he would also take deliberate flights of free association—she saw him stand and stare at a refrigerator handle one night and begin, 'Refrigerator handle—Frigidaire—air-hose—snake. . . . ' It went on for half an hour with incredible quickness. Any object, a refrigerator, a tree, a house, seemed to be to him not only itself but the sum of the associations he could wreathe around it, a microcosm, in fact, and out of these exercises came his symbols and many new word combinations."

Anyone familiar with Arthur Rimbaud's "deliberate derangement of all the senses," Hart Crane's poetry, Yeats's "Magic" (1901), and T. S. Eliot's view of the metaphysicals (1921) can see the widespread acceptance of such a theory of heightening by modern poets. Georges Lemaitre summarizes Rimbaud's techniques in *From Cubism to Surrealism in French Literature* (1947):

> A visionary state cannot be achieved by one who is in a condition of complete mental equilibrium; the spirit must be wrenched from the grip of rational conceptions. The senses, which are the great means of communication with the ordinary world, must be put systematically out of their proper working order: "Le poète se fait voyant par un long, immense, raisonné dérèglement de tous les sens." This is not to be effected by means of artificial devices but simply by forcing the senses into a paroxysm of action exceeding the limits of their normal working power. When the fiery intensity of "toutes les formes d'amour, de souffrance, de folie," has caused a breakdown of our conventional receptive and interpretative mechanism, when the very excess of strain has filled our material nature with numbing "poisons," then only is the mind liberated from all its shackles. Then, even though he may have become a physical wreck, a criminal in the eyes of the world, a being accursed, man at last enters into supreme knowledge; he attains the unknown.

According to Brom Weber's *Hart Crane* (1948), Crane, who was also an early influence on Roethke, had been put on to Rimbaud's techniques by Ezra Pound's "A Study of French Modern Poets" (1918): "Pound's observation that the key to Rimbaud's accomplishment was the utilization of intense emotional feeling, with direct entrance by the poet into the subject as method, undoubtedly was significant to Crane." In "Magic," Yeats associates the style with concepts of a Great Mind and a Great Memory, and Roethke, in phrases reminiscent of Eliot, extends it in "On 'Identity' " to John Donne and the metaphysicals.

The role of poet-as-instrument and the Goethean notion of style coincide, too, with Carl Jung's notions of an "original undivided harmony of plant, animal, man and God," whose restoration might be accomplished through a process of psychological self-realization—an opening of conscious forces to the unconscious so as to avoid a one-sidedness that may contribute to neurosis. This phylogenetic undivided harmony whose loss is symbolized in the Fall is repeated ontogenetically in the lost, individual harmonies of child-hood. Echoing Yeats's notion of a Great Memory, Jung notes in "Psychology and Poetry" (1930) that the great artist touches "that salubrious and redeem-ing psychic depth . . . where all still feel the same vibration, and where, there-fore, the sentiment and action of the individual reach out to all humanity." In the particular case of Roethke, whose return to redeeming self-realization involves a return to childhood, Jung's statement in *The Theory of Psycho-analysis* (1913) is especially apt: "The little world of childhood with its familiar surroundings is a model of the greater world. The more intensively the family has stamped its character upon the child, the more it will tend to feel and see its earlier miniature world again in the bigger world of adult life." But "what youth found and must find outside," Roethke now "in middle life must find within him." Thus, although his search for harmony must be an inner search, as Jung indicates in "Concerning Birth" (1940), an outer in-crease of experience must carry with it the sense of inner expanding spatiality: "Everything which comes from without becomes our own only when we are capable of an inner spaciousness which corresponds to the size of the outer increase. The actual increase in personality is the becoming conscious of a widening, which flows from inner sources." But what Roethke becomes conscious of in *Open House* is not a spaciousness but a widening separation of inner and outer worlds through a failure of language to act properly as a mediator of deeds and rage.

Part of this failure of language is caused by linguistic differences between the internalized, primal, familial world of the greenhouse, Saginaw, and the tradition which Roethke sought to escape in *Open House* and that of Roethke's literary adult life. He focuses on one root of this difference in *Twentieth Century Authors, First Supplement* (1955): "I had no interest in verse after an intense period of pleasure in nursery rhymes in English and German and songs my mother and nurse sang me." The same mixture of English and German sounded in the greenhouse, and Seager notes that the

John Moore School, which Roethke attended for eight years, out of
deference to the district's large German population required students to
spend an hour a day learning German. Yet, though from five to fourteen
years of age he had taken German, Roethke resisted learning it. Seager reports, "He never spoke it except for a few idiomatic phrases he may have
picked up in the greenhouse from the workmen; he could barely read it or
write it. This may have been, with his parents' unspoken consent, some dim,
attenuated hangover of the immigrant's rejection of the Old Country."
Roethke says for *Twentieth Century Authors* that "I really wanted at fifteen
and sixteen, to write a beautiful, a 'chiseled' prose as it was called in those
days" and cites, as possibly the source for Seager's statement, models in
"Stevenson, Pater, Newman, Tomlinson, and those maundering charm boys
known as familiar essayists." In the light of Roethke's defenses of the German character in letters to Dorothy Gordon (1934) and Katharine Stokes
(1939), one might as accurately put down his rejection of German to simple
adolescent rebellion. In either case, the German-American world and basis of
what became his educated Anglo-American language would lead to the kind
of separation between emotions and their expression which Roethke complains of in his first volume.

A second kind of linguistic separation entering *Open House* and con-
tributing more generally to the failure of language is that suggested in Paul
Verlaine's dictum that poets strangle rhetoric. The "nakedness" or "plainness" which Yeats embarks upon in such poems as "A Coat" (1914) and the
"Martian generalities" and abuses of language which Pound complains of in
Homage to Sextus Propertius (1917) and "How to Read" (1928) have their
correspondence in Roethke's "plainness" and calls for precision. Somehow,
words had to be brought out of their embroidered mythologies to reestablish
relations with experience much as, for William Carlos Williams, language's
"lateral sliding" and divorcement from experience had to be overcome. But,
in *Open House,* Roethke seeks to overcome the separation more in the
management of adjectives and the manner of past poets' depiction of experience than by what, in "Marianne Moore" (1931), Williams designates as
her practice of "wiping soiled words or cutting them clean out, removing the
aureoles that have been pasted about them or taking them bodily from greasy
contexts" so that the word stands "crystal clear with no attachments; not
even an aroma." "No Bird," for example, with its strong structural and
linguistic ties to Emily Dickinson appears in Roethke's *Selected Letters*
(1968) after a statement that he had "been reading Emily Dickinson considerably," and, even without such admissions, one senses about many poems in
the volume that their attempts through imitation at precision are but another
move away from primal language.

Moreover, if the practice of poets like Yeats, Pound, Wylie, Auden, Adams, and Dickinson were not enough to warn Roethke of a discrepancy between rhetoric and poetry, his dual capacity as a publicity man and creative writer at Lafayette College from 1931 to 1935 would bring him experientially into the realms both of language's abuses and its clarifications. His letters during these years make this apparent. Their continual preoccupation with exaggeration and self-promotion on the one hand, or, on the other, with cliché, influence, didacticism, dryness, grunt and fart rhythms, precision, concreteness, and syntax illustrates the dichotomy Pound detects in twentieth-century discourse. This dichotomy will be resolved eventually in Roethke's acceptance of the "aggregate self," which "can grow gracefully and beautifully like a tendril, like a flower," but, for the present, as he explains in "On 'Identity' " and as the *Selected Letters* makes very clear, it leads, out of ignorance and a "desire for the essential," into a series of necessary and wilful psychic betrayals.

The particular complaints about language which Roethke registers in *Open House* are severally connected with the volume's overriding effort to appropriate Yeats's "enterprise in walking naked" and keep the "spirit spare." In the title poem, having established "no need for tongue," Roethke opposes the "strict and pure" language of deed to "the lying mouth" and ends by asserting, "Rage warps my clearest cry / To witless agony." He repeats this discrepancy between rage and language in "Silence," where "The spirit crying in a cage / To build a complement to rage" remains undistorted by language, "terribly within the mind." But even when language exists, as in "Orders for the Day" and "The Signals," it may not lead to communication. The first shows "decision's smoking fuse" being smothered by the carelessness of clumsy fingers whose lack of contact with spirit prompts them to "bruise / The Spirit's tender cover." The second asserts, "Sometimes the blood is privileged to guess / The things the eye or hand cannot possess." In "Death Piece," death becomes by extension invention's being completely cut off from the world, and, in "Idyll," a world evolves where all objects are caught up in an other-excluding "self-talk." In "Prognosis," Roethke allies excessive language with spiritual cowardice, and, in "Academic," he makes the growing limpness of style a sign of spiritual degeneration. At the same time, in "Feud," he insists on the need to reject primal language, for "The spirit starves / Until the dead have been subdued." Yet, however close these mutually excluding inner and outer worlds of *Open House* are to a Cartesian subject-object dichotomy or to what, in *Poets of Reality* (1965), J. Hillis Miller calls the dualistic dispute of Romanticism, Roethke's resolution of them in this and his next volume shows them to be not philosophical, but clearly linguistic and psychological.

The techniques in *Open House* which comprise the resolution of these primal and educated worlds are deliberate attempts to submerge the onto-genetic and particular into larger, more universalizing classes. The volume's language, rhythms, and metaphors evince a general avoidance of the idio-syncratic, the specific, the particular, or whatever might be termed the in-dividual. Out of his primal, German-American "gut"-responses, Roethke chooses what can be blurred and warped into an educated, imitative Brahmin diction. As Samuel Johnson's Imlac advises in *Rasselas* (1759), "He does not number the streaks of the tulip, or describe the different shades in the verdure of the forest," but "remarks general properties and large ap-pearances." In the title poem, for instance, adverbs and adjectives which usually capture the individual and which might reveal the poet's backwoodsy, non-English origins appear vague, normative, and impersonal. Roethke's secrets cry "aloud." Had they cried "murder," one might have had a dif-ferent, less controlled condition for the heart's keeping "open house." Here truths are "all foreknown," anguish is "self-revealed," and language "strict and pure." Only at the poem's end with "lying mouth," "clearest cry," and "witless agony" does a wave of modifiers collect and, although descriptive, none is particular enough to alter the poem's generalizing tone.

In poems like "Epidermal Macabre" and "Prayer," this submergence of individualizing particulars extends to Roethke's willingness to "dispense / With false accoutrements of sense" and value sight above all other senses because it is least tied to the individualizing properties of the body. In *Twentieth Century Authors,* Roethke reveals in an encounter with Robert Hillyer some of the sense of cultural inferiority which contributes to the normative language. He goes to meet the poet "complete with fur coat and a fancy suit" and adds, in a telling aside, "those Harvards weren't going to have it over me." The same sense of inferiority appears in a letter to Rolfe Humphries (1934) describing a meeting with Louise Bogan: "I was like a country boy at his first party,—such an oaf, such a boob, such a blockhead. I don't think I was ever much worse." His recurrent hatred of his "epidermal dress," his wanting to be with the fish, the bears, the slugs, conveys a comple-mentary, more personal embarrassment with his physique that might also have contributed to his tendency away from self.

Literary justification for this tendency to blur individual responses into normative language is offered in Genevieve Taggard's anthology of metaphysi-cal poetry, *Circumference* (1929). In "A Greenhouse Eden" (1965), Louis L. Martz mentions its importance to *Open House,* although as early as 1934 Roethke was discrediting it. The book presents Dickinson and Donne as the twin beacons to guide any would-be metaphysical poet safely into port. In delineating their attractiveness, Taggard notes: "Ideas being for this tempera-ment as real as grass blades or locomotives, the poet's imagination is always riding the two horses in the circus, Idea and Fact; they gallop neck and neck in his work, he has a genius for both the concrete word and the dazzling concept." But more importantly, in a skeleton metaphor foreshadowing Roethke's in "Open House," she stresses impersonality: "To give an idea no form but itself, to show it as organic by an inner music, as if the bones of a skeleton were singing in their own rhythm—that is the technical obsession of the metaphysical poet." Tied to the impersonality is compression: "The wit, the power to make an epigram which Donne's age so loved, is all in Emily Dickinson." This compression, this seeing like William Blake the world in a grain of sand, is something which remains constant in Roethke's writing. Later, detailing for Ann Winslow's *Trial Balances* (1935) the qualities she most prized in Roethke's verse, Bogan chose for special emphasis the same, impersonal epigram-making power reduced now to epithet: "His feeling for epithet is also marked. The gift of poetic epithet, in a high degree, is comparatively rare. Such a gift presupposes sensibilities beyond the average in the poet, since the good epithet is the result of a true and hard impact between the thing felt or seen and the poet's natural power of emotion and perception." But the change to epithet in no way decreases the objectivity of the style.

Similarly normalized to the point of prompting William Meredith's statement in "A Steady Storm of Correspondences" (1965) that "the issues of the poems were resolved by poetic formulas" are the volume's rhythms and metaphors. Roethke did not yet understand Donne's practice of counterpointing speech rhythms against the normal stresses of iambic verse nor had he moved into what, in *The Forgotten Language* (1951), another Bennington colleague, Erich Fromm, calls "symbolic language." Although influenced by Taggard's view of the two horses of Idea and Fact, there is in the poetry no widespread expression of "inner experience as if it were a sensory experience, as if it were something we were doing or something that was done to us in the world of things." The world outside is not yet sufficiently a symbol of the world inside, "a symbol for our souls and our mind." Nor has there occurred, as Jung indicates in self-realization there should, any sense of increasing inner spatiality to accompany the outer increase of experience. The blurring of the individual into the universal on this deliberate, public level precludes the kind of inner self-discovery which permits for the formation of such symbolic language. This language, which Fromm roots in an Eliot-like "affinity between an emotion or thought, on the one hand, and a sensory experience, on the other" has a transcultural commonality which permits, when Roethke moves into it, for the discovery of the universal from within, from the particular or local. "Mid-Country Blow," which, with its regression into the womb, looks forward to later poems like "Big Wind" and "The Storm," or "The Premonition," which prefigures Roethke's treatment of his father in "The

Lost Son" and "Otto," or "On the Road to Woodlawn" and "The Heron,"
which increase significantly the number of concretely descriptive adjectives
and adverbs, indicate the direction of Roethke's next volume, but in *Open
House,* he engages upon wit as the exclusive device to mediate metaphoric
tenor and vehicle, inner and outer worlds, and primal and educated languages.

In poems like "Dolor," Roethke carries this preoccupation with the failure
of language into *The Lost Son* (1948). Here his awareness of the failure's
source in the giving way of primal to educated language is translated into the
deadly "inexorable sadness of pencils" and "dust from the walls." This dust is
"more dangerous than silica" in shaping the world's "duplicate grey standard
faces." Auden is still apparent in the language of the poem's closing line, but
the awareness of the evil of "the trivia of the institution" makes possible
Roethke's abandonment of the universalizing detail and his move to symbolic
language and the psychic corrections which the volume attempts. Part of the
move to symbolic language is tied to an acceptance of Rilke's belief in a
useful, unified life-death existence which permits Roethke to abandon the
rejection of his primal world evident in poems like "Feud." In "On
'Identity,'" Roethke associates his acceptance of "the great dead" to a re-
mark which John Peale Bishop made during a writers conference at Olivet
College in 1940, but which took Roethke "some years to learn": "You're
impassioned, but wrong. The dead can help us." Part is tied to writing techniques derived from D. H. Lawrence and Williams, and part to the personal
encouragement of Kenneth Burke. In the long poems which comprise the
volume's final section and which, for Roethke and critics alike, constitute its
major accomplishment, additional influences of nursery rhyme, Elizabethan
rant, Gerard Manley Hopkins, James Joyce, and E. E. Cummings are present.

Seager dates Roethke's interest in Rilke to the arrival of Philip Shelley at
Penn State in 1939 and a joint course Shelley and Roethke taught in Rilke,
Yeats, and Auden. As Rilke explained his view of existence in a letter to his
Polish translator, Witold von Hulewicz (1925): "Death is the *side of life* that
is turned away from us: we must try to achieve the fullest consciousness of
our existence, which is at home in *the two unseparated realms, inexhaustibly
nourished by both.* . . . The true figure of life extends through *both* domains,
the blood of the mightiest circulation drives through *both: there is neither a
here nor a beyond, but the great unity,* in which those creatures that surpass
us, the 'angels,' are at home." In translating this belief into images of subsurface, surface, and oversurface, Roethke adds a psychological vitality indebted
in part to Lawrence, whose work he had encountered at the University of
Michigan in 1930. Like Rilke, Lawrence believed in a unified, life-death
existence. In *Etruscan Places* (1928), he had written: "And death, to the
Etruscan, was a pleasant continuance of life, with jewels and wine and flutes

playing for the dance." This continuance past death and "non-existence to far oblivion" is a preoccupation of Lawrence's *Last Poems* (1932).

But what Roethke publicly acknowledges in "Some Remarks on Rhythm" (1960) as the influence of Lawrence on him is more technical than ideological. The devices of enumeration and of varying line length which these poems use, he designates as "the favorite devices of the more irregular poem" and allies them to Whitman and Lawrence: "It was Lawrence, a master of this kind of poem (I think I quote him more or less exactly) who said, 'It all depends on the pause, the natural pause.' In other words, the breath unit, the language that is natural to the immediate thing, the particular emotion." Yet, Lawrence's Introduction to the American edition of *New Poems* (1918), wherein he writes of his indebtedness to Whitman and which, along with Williams, furnishes the Roethkean terminology, also makes clear that poetry is self-expression and that free verse, as "the soul and the mind and body surging at once," cannot leave ideology out. Louise Bogan, whose judgments Roethke had courted since the thirties, in reviewing Lawrence's *Selected Poems* (1948), tellingly attributes to the English poet a revival of Nature poetry in a nonsentimental and a nonshamefaced way, and one does sense that Roethke's handling of nature is closer to the Lawrence of *Birds, Beasts and Flowers* (1928) than to any other modern poet. The sense is even strengthened when reading his letter to Burke detailing his project for a Houghton Mifflin Literary Fellowship Award (1945). In it, he describes the greenhouse poems which comprise the opening section of *The Lost Son* in the mixture of nature, eroticism, and mysticism common to Lawrence: "The poems done so far are not sufficiently related and do not show the full erotic and even religious significance that I sense in a big greenhouse: a kind of man-made Avalon, Eden, or paradise."

What Roethke wished publicly to have acknowledged about the Williams influence upon him is similarly misleading. In objecting to a comment in *100 American Poems* (1948) that he "derived his undressed and deceptively simple style from the cross-grained imagist, William Carlos Williams," Roethke told Selden Rodman: "I do owe him a debt for jibing me in conversation and by letter to get out of small forms; but his own work I don't know as well as I should. . . . His (Wms.) rhythms are more staccato, more broken, seems to me." Yet, in a letter to Williams (1944), he had acknowledged some affinity: "Anything with images equals Imagism equals Old Hat. Oh well, you know all that better than I; have seen it, have been fighting it." And in a letter to Burke (1946), he admitted to a Williams-like literalness: "Do I betray myself as too literal? But I try to be true to the actual (be exact) and also to get the widest yet most honest symbolical richness too." Moreover, Jackson wrote Seager in this connection: "In rough-draft the long poems appeared to be in free verse (or rather, a line closer to what William Carlos Williams calls *versos sueltos,* loose-limber verse with enough exactness and repetition in measure to avoid free-verse monotony"[)] .

Williams had hit upon the technique of *versos sueltos* after 1923 in an effort to capture in his writing not the mere copy of life, but art's inner life. As he notes in his *Autobiography* (1951), "It is to make, out of the imagination, something not at all a copy of nature, a thing advanced and apart from it." But for Roethke who is given to mysticism, this imitation is involved with a metaphysical introspection not common to Williams. In fact, Williams' Introduction to *The Wedge* (1944) insists, "Let the metaphysical take care of itself, the arts have nothing to do with it." Seager suggests a second personality difference in Roethke's summary of a first meeting with Williams in 1942: "We had a powerful lack of interest in each other's poetry," and one suspects, as Roethke suggests in a letter to Williams enclosing "The Lost Son" (1946), that the connection between the two poets lies in Williams' lifelong courtship of a natural American language and metrical breath unit. Roethke was fond of quoting Bennington president Lewis Jones's statement that Roethke was "a grass roots American with classic tastes," and, in the Williams letter, he writes: "But here's a long one which I think is the best I've done so far. It's written, as you'll see right away, for the ear and not the eye. It's written to be heard. And if you don't think it's got the accent of native American speech, your name ain't W. C. Williams, I say belligerently." Yet, even here there were differences. Williams' view of language as "bricklaying" where words are solidified against translucency and connotation much in the way pigment was solidified by the cubists is different from Roethke's Yeatsian view of words as a means for the evocation of memory.

Nor can one minimize the enthusiasm of Burke in the writing of these poems. Roethke was bothered by various personal, cultural, and professional insecurities throughout most of his life, and the enthusiasm of an eminent, hard-nosed critic like Burke for poems which began to open the childhood German-American world Roethke thought in his first volume to shun out of embarrassment would permit the poet to chance the self-expression of Lawrence and risk even greater entry into this world. Though perhaps not as directly seminal, since the new style of the greenhouse poems had begun to evolve in such works as "City Limits" (1941), "Germinal" (1943), and "The Minimals" before Roethke's arrival at Bennington, it was, nevertheless, important. Seager reports that Burke came into Roethke's room one day in 1945 and, hearing two greenhouse poems, reacted by saying, "Boy, you've hit it." His demands for more produced a series of poems which Roethke published in 1946 and led to Roethke's admission in the Williams letter (1946) that the two were greatly responsible for the new style. In a separate letter to Burke (1946), Roethke confesses: "But my real point is: Your belief and interest in the piece has set me up very much." Yet, Roethke's objection in a 1949 letter to Burke about his trying to make out of the long poems "a kind of *collage*" and his insistence to Rodman and others on the poems' seeming "to come from a tapping of an older memory—something that dribbled out of the unconscious, as it were, the racial memory or whatever it's called" suggest a degree of initial misreading even in Burke toward surface and a Williams-like poetics.

In "Open Letter," Roethke cites as additional "ancestors" of these poems: "German and English folk literature, particularly Mother Goose; Elizabethan and Jacobean drama, especially the songs and rants; the Bible; Blake and Traherne; Dürer. . . . Rhythmically, it's the spring and rush of the child I'm after—and Gammar Gurton's concision: *mütterkin*'s wisdom." He was doubtlessly put on to these "ancestors" and rhythms by Hopkins' famous Preface to his *Poems* (1918). In that preface, noting the nature and history of Sprung Rhythm, Hopkins writes: "Sprung Rhythm is the most natural of things. For (1) it is the rhythm of common speech and of written prose, when rhythm is perceived in them. (2) It is the rhythm of all but the most monotonously regular music, so that in the words of choruses and refrains and in songs written closely to music it arises. (3) It is found in nursery rhymes, weather saws, and so on; because, however these may have been once made in running rhythm, the terminations having dropped off by the change of language, the stresses come together and so the rhythm is sprung. (4) It arises in common verse when reversed or counterpointed, for the same reason." Joyce's *Finnegans Wake,* Bogan would have it, is also important. Seager reports that "It is her opinion that it was Joyce, not Yeats, the verbal exuberance of the Joyce of *Ulysses* and *Finnegans Wake* that influenced Ted in *The Lost Son.*"

Certainly, Bogan's review of *Praise to the End!* (1952) sets up with words like "nonsense" and "gibberish" echoes of her review of *Finnegans Wake* (1939). Of Roethke, she writes: "But it is witty nonsense and effective gibberish, since the poet's control over this difficult material is always formal; he knows exactly when to increase and when to decrease pressure, and he comes to a stop just before the point of monotony is reached. Behind Roethke's method exists the example of Joyce, but Roethke has invented a symbolism, in his searching out these terrors, marginal to our consciousness, that is quite his own." Of Joyce, she notes: It is "not gibberish unless it wants to be. It has rules and inventions. . . . It is related to what Panurge called the 'puzzlatory,' and it is cousin to the language of E. Lear, L. Carroll, and writers of nonsense verse in general." Yet the device of "paranomasia," which she mentions as Joyce's peculiar contribution and which involves a great deal of translingual punning, is not used by Roethke, and one feels more the nursery rhyme opening of *A Portrait of the Artist as a Young Man* (1916) than the dream language of *Finnegans Wake.* Roethke seems to have sensed this difference, too, in a letter to Burke (1949) disowning a connection between his evocations of the wholeness of childhood and Joyce's dreamlife evocations of a racial past: "Off-hand, I don't know anyone who's tried this before, with any success. Joyce is something else .... Also Faulkner in *As I Lay Dying."*

The kind of verbal displacement which occurs in the volume's final section happens in the manner which, in "Emily Dickinson" (1962), Northrop Frye describes as happening in her poetry: "In popular poetry there is a clearly marked rhythm and the words chosen to fill it up give approximately the intended meaning, but there is no sense of any *mot juste* or uniquely appropriate word.... For a great many of her poems she has provided alternative words, phrases, even whole lines, as though the rhythm, like a figured bass in music, allowed the editor or reader to establish his own text." In "The Long Alley," "Tricksy comes and tricksy goes" owes more to the rhythms of the saw "Handsome is as handsome does" than to any sophisticated paranomasia. The same is true of "For the waltz of To, / The pinch of Where" in "The Shape of the Fire," which owe their being more to the Cummings of "anyone lived in a pretty how town" (1940) than to Joyce. The child swing rhythms of the Cummings poem are later modified into the jumping rope rhythms of Roethke's "I Need, I Need," and, contrary to Seager's contention that Cummings had no literary influence on Roethke despite his being the only poet of Roethke's contemporaries he always praised in the privacy of his notebooks, in this matter of verbal displacement along a figured bass Cummings proves, indeed, an influence and able most "to blow up the language," for as Roethke repeatedly insists, the key to the structure of the volume's long poems lies not in the narrative sense but in the rhythms.

The poems of the opening section of *The Lost Son* define the elements of Roethkean existence. Thoughts rise as images from the unconscious where, having been accorded cognition, they return. Submerged there, they collect about them other experiences and sensations and, with new accretions, on occasion erupt again into consciousness. This psychological approximation of the Rilkean life-death cycle creates a new language of image rather than of word where slime represents subsurface and air, consciousness. The Rilkean "angel" who inhabits the fulness of both worlds is replaced, as in Yeats's poetry, by the Roethkean "symbol." In the symbols of the new poems, "Cuttings" establishes that birth is life coming through the slime. With strong phallic imagery, the reproduction of "Cuttings Later" pulls the worlds of plant and man together. "Root Cellar" posits a cemeterial slime where things refuse to die and go on living a perverse, subsurface life. "Forcing House" enlarges the unity of "Cuttings Later" to machines by imaging the steam pipes that keep flowers alive as a pulse. "Weed Puller" betrays perhaps most patently the cycle's Rilkean influence. The speaker tugging all day under the concrete benches feels the intrusion of perverse, subsurface life rather than the joys of blossom. As in Rilke, death becomes an aspect of life, but Rilke's death, which seems more attractive than life, differs from this poem's less attractive world. The swamp of "Moss-Gathering" becomes a sanctuary for perverse life which thrives to become eventually coal and opposes the greenhouse of "Big Wind," which hoves the evils of the world like a ship bearing souls to heaven. The poem leads to the image of the florist in "Old Florist" as a magician, as a redeemer, like Jung's poet, pulling blossoms into being, and of the three ancient ladies of "Frau Bauman, Frau Schmidt, and Frau Schwartze" as three fates.

The very cyclical nature of this existence creates a flow which opposes the arresting confrontations of *Open House.* There is little attempt in these poems to put on form *ab exteriori* and, by imposing form, encounter "the dullness, confusion or remplissage or the 'falling between two stools' " that Pound indicates can occur. The natural breath unit is used; the fusion of tenor and vehicle exists on a preconscious level. In accepting the descriptive language positing the objects, the reader accepts the poems' implicit metaphors. There is, as a consequence, a clarity that marks the group as a whole and which manages, by keeping to basic emotions and experiences of birth, death, and physical and spiritual transfigurations, a commonality through particulars which Fromm assigns to symbolic language and Yeats to symbol. But the kind of Lawrentian oneing, which now occurs in the conscious or subconscious prior to a poem's start rather than at its close, requires a new kind of nakedness if the artist is to remain precise. Stephen Spender writes of this need in "The Objective Ego" (1965): " 'Separateness' like 'swaying' is a word that bears much weight of meaning in his poems. It is not the separateness of things from one another which concerns him so deeply, but to see their separateness from himself." The mystic who has oned himself and world lacks the aesthetic distance with which to describe the world. Without it, there can be no adequte outlet for communication and, as Spender indicates, Roethke, at such times, "becomes the egotist who burdens the reader with his problems." Jackson reports that during the years when Roethke developed his symbolic language, rather than stripping descriptive adjectives he was "popping out of his clothes, wandering around the cottage naked for a while, then dressing slowly, four or five times a day." Seager remarks, "There are some complex 'birthday-suit' meanings here, the ritual of starting clean like a baby, casting one's skin like a snake, and then donning the skin again. It was not exhibitionism. No one saw. It was all a kind of magic." These magic rituals which make physical Yeats's metaphor of walking naked serve also the symbolic purpose of separating Roethke from the skin of his world so that he can with literalness reproduce that world.

As the volume's opening section establishes this cycle of perverse and blooming life, the long poems of the book establish the cycle's inner time dimension. In so doing, they allow a spatiality absent from *Open House,* wherein adult worlds can be shaped to the images of a child. This shaping which permits Roethke to merge his German-American childhood and his Anglo-American adult world lessens the sense of mutually excluding inner and outer worlds unmediated by language. There are no two circus horses galloping neck and neck and no complaints of emotions' being warped or trapped within the mind. In fact, the flow of language is such as to suggest that the poet is an instrument of what Rilke called the glances and gestures that become blood within the writer and which now will out. The ease at which images arise and mediate between cultures opposes the earlier anguish at blurring the individual into the species, the ontogenetic into the phylogenetic. A sense of joy appears similar to that which in *Psychological Types* (1921) Jung assigns generally to metaphors of "childlikeness": "The feeling of bliss accompanies all those moments which have the character of flowing life, . . . 'when it goes of itself,' where there is no longer any need to manufacture all sorts of wearisome conditions by which joy or pleasure might be stimulated. The age of childhood is the unforgettable token of this joy, which, undismayed by things without, streams all-embracing from within." Thus, Roethke's placement of easeful self-expression into the " 'as if' of the child's world," nursery-rhyme, and fairy tale takes on precedence. In the same way, his insistence in letters and essays that the world of these long poems is sexual in no way negates its childlikeness, for, as Jung indicates in "Experiences Concerning the Psychic Life of the Child" (1910), "Fairy-stories seem to be the myths of childhood, and therefore, among other things, they contain the mythology which the child has woven around the sexual processes. The fascination which the poetic charm of the fairy-story has for adults is also perhaps due not least to the fact that some of these old theories are still alive in the unconscious."

Roethke's refusal in "Open Letter" to be "some kind of over-size aeolian harp upon which strange winds play uncouth tunes" forces him to admit to some consciousness in the writing of the poems. But even if he had not, one has only to follow his use of "sleep song" through the pages of "Where Knock Is Open Wide" and note the precise way "away" (hell) is distinguished from "somewhere else" (heaven) to believe the careful outlines which Jackson reports Roethke constructed before beginning the poems. Still, in reading them, one realizes that even with these outlines and Roethke's explanations as guide the poems are unintelligible. Part of the unintelligibility comes from the nature of their "symbolic language." Symbols of the unconscious have always bipolar potential, at times meaning a thing and its opposite coevally. Often explications that appeal to a reader's cognitive faculties do not account for this bipolar tendency or for the rhythms and evocative situations which insinuate themselves deeply into any response. Meredith allows that "the obscurity is that of a lucid dream, where only the causes and connections, not the facts or events, are in doubt," and, in "The Anguish of Concreteness" (1965), W. D. Snodgrass, adding his admiration for the originality of the poems, feels the need to admit as well that "Even now, more than twelve years since those poems appeared, I do not feel that I really understand them, or feel certain how ultimately successful they are." Similarly, in "The Power of Sympathy" (1965), Roy Harvey Pearce ventures: "In a sense, they are not poems but rather pre-poems; so that the reader, working through them, must bring his own capacities as protopoet to bear on them. In effect, the reader *completes* them. One can hardly talk about these poems, or in terms of them. One can only try to talk through them—which perhaps is a way, a way we too much neglect, of learning, all over again, to talk."

The attempts of these critics to come to grips with the unintelligibility of the poems along with other tendencies to misread them provide some insight on how the poems may work on readers generally. Their constructed self-expressions of the wholeness of the poet through a recovery of childhood become evocations for the reader's own tendency toward wholeness. Though of a similar kind, the two tendencies may remain completely independent of each other. In *The Craft of Fiction* (1921), Percy Lubbock describes this phenomenon as it affects the reader's creation, in his reading, of a novel different from the author's. In the same way, the poems, by allowing something akin to the "self-talk" of "Idyll," assert a failure of language to mediate different from that of *Open House.* To the degree that poems succeed, words function much as they do in Yeats's "Magic," not to communicate directly between self and other but to evoke images out of the Great Mind and Great Memory which the reader can feel. What we have in the long poems, then, is intersubjectivity used for communication. What of childhood overlaps in a reader and poet gets mediated; what does not gets lost. This intersubjectivity is possible because at the root of the Goethean notion of style is a connaturality of subjectivity and the reality which poetic knowledge has caused the poet to see. They are alike in nature and essence. Thus, when a poem reveals the inner side of things, it reveals the inner depth of self, and the self arrives by the revelation at spiritual communion with being. In such a poetics which tends to slight the reader, the problems of language as communication become subordinated to the reader's sensitivity in translating accurately the emotions set off by the word. For complete interaction, his sensitivity to symbolic language must equal the poet's.

The ten poems which Roethke adds to complete the sequence, extending its range backward and forward, begin to show the strain of invention which set in after *The Lost Son.* Martz complains that the poems of the next volume "too often destroy themselves by violent experiments in a Tom o'Bedlam style," and Meredith wishes to dismiss *Praise to the End!* as Roethke's least successful collection, commanding admiration only "as a feat of exploration." Rather than rhythms and a precision to capture the movements of the mind in form, one senses, in its mechanical arrangments and repetition, design as an overriding principle. Simple transpositions increase as rescuing devices for cliché. "Once upon a tree / I came upon a time," for example, is saved by such a device. Likewise, there is a growing literariness in the number of lines and half-lines echoing past poets, Dr. Seuss, and nursery rhyme. Evidently a new blockage has occurred. Either, as Snodgrass conjectures, the ventures into the incredible inner landscapes of self-expression produced a fear and a "need to step back and regather his forces" or the consternation at the poems' inability to communicate forced Roethke into more traditional forms as a remedy. Yet, it was not until "The Dance" (1952) that the extremes of such a remedy occur and one gets for Roethke's educated Anglo-American language the same kind of interiorization and ease that one encountered in the greenhouse poems. The poem came after "a longish dry period" in which the poet felt he was through. Roethke reports in "On 'Identity' ": "Suddenly, in the early evening, the poem, 'The Dance,' started and finished itself in a very short time—say thirty minutes, maybe in the greater part of an hour, it was all done. I felt, I *knew,* I had hit it. . . . But at the same time I had, as God is my witness, the actual sense of a Presence—as if Yeats himself were in that room."

The poem begins significantly with the poet learning to dance alone, moving in what became the other parts of "Four for Sir John Davies" to a living partner, then to embrace the dead, and finally into an all-embracing Dantean light. That Roethke should feel the need to sense a Presence is explained by Jung in "The Phenomenology of the Spirit in Fairytales" (1948) in the endopsychic automatisms which appear in hopeless and desperate situations from which only profound reflection or a lucky idea, compensating the deficiency, can extricate the self. These endopsychic automatisms or personified thoughts come often in the shapes of sagacious and helpful old men. Williams' poetry is filled with them, either as his grandmother or as representations of himself at various points of his life, and like Williams, Roethke seems fated in his work to go on discovering and to evince an inability at filling in those territories he discovers. In *The Theory of Psychoanalysis,* Jung writes about this need to make peace with an educated language as well as a childhood language. He details the dangers of one's remaining perpetually a child, for without such an integration that would be, in effect, what artistically Roethke would be doing. Jung states: "We know that the first impressions of childhood cannot be lost, but cling to the individual accompanying him throughout his whole life, and that certain educative influences which are equally indestructible are capable of restricting the individual within certain bounds for life. Under these conditions it is no wonder and in fact even a frequent experience that conflicts break out between that personality which was shaped by education and other influences of the childhood's milieu and the true individual line of life." Jung singles out for this specific conflict people especially "who are ordained to lead an independent, creative life."

That this educated language should be so indebted to Yeats has become an embarrassment to Roethke critics. These critics are bothered, as well, by Roethke's notion of "aggregate voice," upon which he comments in "On 'Identity,' " and which challenges the unified voice of Romanticism. He quotes his poem, "A Light Breather," to show how voice takes and embraces its surroundings, "never wishing itself away." It is both the self perceived in *Open House* and the operative, perceiving "I." The discovery of this perceiving "I" is made by the kind of playing-at-roles which George Herbert Mead encourages in *Mind, Self, and Society* (1934). Being quite distinguishable from the body and contrary to its metaphor of a blossoming flower, this "I" is not to be found in any one shape or poem but is the spirit which infuses the whole. The flower metaphor is simply to give the concept comprehensibility, to bring the symbolic language of the poetry into Roethke's criticism. Snodgrass, who in his essay accepts the literalness of a form, would have readers see Roethke's poem, "The Kitty-Cat Bird," as the history of his voice's being swallowed into Yeats's. The acceptance forces him to distort the poem's moral. Consistent with Roethke's "aggregate voice," it encourages the bird's cat mews, jay grates, and mouse squeaks rather than an assignment of self to a single role, be it in or out of a real cat. Such assignment is to "up and die."

This notion of a unified voice which is at odds with the flexible listening of Goethean style requires an authoritative language Roethke never possessed. Always the country boy, the oaf, the boob, the pot poet, Roethke could do no better linguistically than to become a ventriloquist of those voices approved by his contemporaries. Even here, as John Crowe Ransom notes in "On Theodore Roethke's 'In a Dark Time' " (1961), he was not completely successful. Ransom argues that despite Roethke's "reference to Yeats, who has influenced him," Roethke remains "original, and quickly reasserts his own voice in paying tribute to the other poet." Yet, in the very act of ventriloquy which supplies him with a voice for his adult emotions, Roethke was able to set off and channel an energy which depth psychologists claim America creates. Emanating from the tensions produced by the distance between the high level of her conscious culture and an unmediated unconscious primitive landscape, this energy provides her inhabitants with a spirit of enterprise and enthusiasm which Europeans still in possession of ancestor spirits lack. In the case of Roethke, as in the cases of the immigrants whom H. L. Mencken celebrates in "The Anglo-Saxon" (1923), the energy, translated into the cultural distance between the language of an Anglo-American conscious culture and an unmediated European earthiness, provides avenues of cultural, technological, and scientific growth. On occasion, and particularly in *The Lost Son,* Roethke was able with such energy to achieve a voice, a rhyme, a line, a poem that redirected and enlivened American letters. Regardless of whether or not it was his, the effect, like that voice of the prudent kitty-cat bird, was to exact from the failures of language something that would lead him not to obliteration but to psychic and artisitic growth.

Delmore Schwartz

The Cunning and the Craft of the Unconscious and the Preconscious

It is sufficiently clear by now that Theodore Roethke is a very important poet. It is also more than likely that his reputation among readers of poetry is based, for the most part, upon the extraordinary lyrics in his second and third volumes. These poems appear, at first glance, to be uncontrollable and subliminal outcries, the voices of roots, stones, leaves, logs, small birds; and they also resemble the songs in Shakespearean plays, Ophelia's songs perhaps most of all. This surface impression is genuine and ought not to be disregarded. But it is only the surface, however moving, and as such, it can be misleading or superficial. The reader who supposes that Roethke is really a primitive lyric poet loses or misses a great deal. Perhaps the best way to define the substance of Roethke's poetry is to quote Valéry's remarkable statement that the nervous system is the greatest of all poems.

The enchanted depths beneath the chanting surface become more recognizable when the reader goes through this new collection [*Words for the Wind*] with care from beginning to end. Throughout his work, Roethke uses a variety of devices with the utmost cunning and craft to bring the unconscious to the surface of articulate expression. But he avoids the danger and the

From *Poetry: A Magazine of Verse,* 94 (June 1959), 203-5. Copyright © 1963 by Delmore Schwartz. Reprinted by permission of Kenneth A. Schwartz.

temptation—which is greater for him than for most poets—of letting this attentiveness to the depths of experience become glib and mechanical, a mere formula for lyricism, which, being willed as a formula, would lose its genuineness and spontaneity. Roethke's incantatory lyrics are not, as they may first seem, all alike; on the contrary, each of them has a uniqueness and individuality.

In a like way, when, in his latest poems, Roethke seems to be imitating not only the manner but the subject-matter of Yeats—and even the phrasing—this too may very well be misleading if it is taken as *merely* imitation: for, first of all, it is paradoxical and true that the most natural and frequent path to true originality, for most good poets, is through imitating the style of a very great poet; secondly, Roethke has begun to imitate Yeats in mid-career, when he is at the height of his powers; and finally, since Yeats is a very different kind of poet than Roethke, the imitation is itself a feat of the imagination: Yeats discovered the concreteness and colloquialism which made him a very great poet only after many phases of vagueness, meandering through the long Celtic twilight; while Roethke's mastery of concreteness of image and thing has served him in good stead from the very start. It is likely enough that the chief reason Roethke has followed Yeats's later style has been to guard against the deadly habit of self-imitation which has paralyzed some of the best poets in English—from Wordsworth to Edwin Arlington Robinson—soon after they enjoyed—at long last—the natural and longed-for recognition of the readers of poetry, after decades of misunderstanding, abuse, and very often the scorn of established critics.

If we compare one of Roethke's new, Yeatsian poems with the kind of poem which it appears to echo and imitate, we can hardly fail to discover not only the differences between the two writers, but something about all of Roethke's poems and about Yeats also.

Here is Roethke in his most Yeatsian phase: this is a stanza from a poem called "The Pure Fury":

> The pure admire the pure and live alone;
> I love a woman with an empty face.
> Parmenides put nothingness in place;
> She tries to think and it flies loose again.
> How slow the changes of a golden mean:
> Great Boehme rooted all in yes and no;
> At times my darling squeaks in pure Plato.

And here is a stanza from "Among School Children," one of the best of all poems of the language, which I quote for close reading, though it is or should be familiar to all readers of poetry:

> Plato thought nature but a spume that plays
> Upon a ghostly paradigm of things;
> Solider Aristotle played the taws
> Upon the bottom of a king of kings;
> World-famous golden-thighed Pythagoras
> Fingered upon a fiddle-stick of strings
> What a star sang and careless Muses heard:
> Old clothes upon old sticks to scare a bird.

The attitude and emotion in the latter poem is precisely the opposite of Roethke's; for Yeats, in this poem, as in so many of his later poems is full of a *contemptus mundi,* a scorn of nature, a detestation of history, which has left him an old man, however gifted: he too like the scarecrow face of the Leda-like beauty with whom he had been in love, has been by "the honey of generation betrayed." And this is why he ends his poem by saying: "How shall we know the dancer from the dance?", a Heraclitean statement that all is process and nothing is reality, except, as in other poems, the frozen artificial reality of Byzantium. And his poem is affirmative only in the sense of confronting despair and death: it is very close to Valéry's "La Cimitière Marin," where existence itself and the mind of the poet seem the sole flaw in the pure diamond of being, so that Valéry's affirmation too is a hardly more than "Il faut tenter de vivre" and he too is appalled by the reality of process and unable to believe in another reality.

Roethke is capable of far greater affirmation—which is not to say that he is, as yet, as good as Yeats and Valéry, but that he is original and important enough to be compared to both poets, and to be regarded as having his own uniqueness. Thus he concludes this, one of his most Yeatsian poems, with the stanza:

> Dream of a woman, and a dream of death;
> The light air takes my being's breath away;
> I look on white and it turns into gray—
> When will that creature give me back my breath?
> I live near the abyss, I hope to stay
> Until my eyes look at a brighter sun
> As the thick shade of the long night comes on.

And it is worth adding that the difficulty of affirmation and hope, and the reality of the abyss have become more and more clear, more and more appalling, for poets alive today, as for all of us, than they were for Yeats when he wrote "Among School Children," and for Valéry when he wrote "La Cimitière Marin."

Stanley Kunitz

Roethke: Poet of Transformations

In the myth of Proteus we are told that at midday he rose from the flood and slept in the shadow of the rocks of the west. Around him lay the monsters of the deep, whom he was charged with tending. He was famous for his gift of prophecy, but it was a painful art, which he was reluctant to employ. The only way anyone could compel him to foretell the future was by pouncing on him while he slept in the open. It was in order to escape the necessity of prohesying that he changed his shape, from lion to serpent to panther to swine to running water to fire to leafy tree—a series of transformations that corresponds with the seasons of the sacred king in his passage from birth to death. If he saw that his struggles were useless, he resumed his ordinary appearance, spoke the truth and plunged back into the sea.

A lifework that embodied the metamorphic principle was abruptly terminated on August 1, 1963, when Theodore Roethke died, in his fifty-fifth year, while swimming at Bainbridge Island, Washington. He was the first American bardic poet since Whitman who did not spill out in prolix and shapeless vulgarity, for he had cunning to match his daemonic energy and he had schooled himself so well in the formal disciplines that he could turn even his stammerings into art. If the transformations of his experience resist division into mineral, vegetable, and animal categories, it is because the levels are continually overlapped, intervolved, in the manifold tissue. Roethke's imagination is populated with shapeshifters, who turn into the protagonists of his poems. Most of these protagonists are aspects of the poet's own being, driven to know itself and yet appalled by the terrible necessity of self-knowledge; assuming every possible shape in order to find the self and to escape the finding; dreading above all the state of annihilation, the threat of non-being; and half-yearning at the last for the oblivion of eternity, the union of the whole spirit with the spirit of the whole universe.

Roethke's first book, *Open House* (1941), despite its technical resourcefulness in the deft probings for a style, provided only a few intimations of what was to develop into his characteristic idiom. The title poem, in its oracular end-stopping and its transparency of language, can serve as prologue to the entire work:

From *The New Republic,* CLII (January 23, 1965), 23-29. Reprinted by permission of *The New Republic,* © 1965, Harrison-Blaine of New Jersey, Inc.

My truths are all foreknown,
This anguish self-revealed. . . .

Myself is what I wear:
I keep the spirit spare.

Perhaps the finest poem in this first volume is "Night Journey," in which the poet, telling of a train ride back to his native Michigan, announces his life-long loyalty to what he never tired of describing, even if somewhat sardon-ically on occasion, as the American heartland. The poem opens:

Now as the train bears west,
Its rhythm rocks the earth . . .

—how important that verb of rocking is to become!—and it ends:

I stay up half the night
To see the land I love.

The middle of the poem is occupied by a quatrain that prefigures one of his typical patterns of response:

Full on my neck I feel
The straining at a curve;
My muscles move with steel,
I wake in every nerve.

Some thirty years later—he seemed never to forget an experience—in the first of his "Meditations of an Old Woman," the old woman being presumably his mother when she is not Roethke himself, he was to offer, through the medium of her voice recalling a bus ride through western country, a recapitu-lation of that same sensation: "taking the curves." His imagination was not conceptual but kinesthetic, stimulated by nerve-ends and muscles, and even in its wildest flights localizing the tension when the curve is taken. This is precisely what Gerard Manley Hopkins meant when, in one of his letters, he spoke of the "isolation of the hip area." The metamorphosis of the body begins in the isolation of the part.

Another poem in *Open House,* entitled "The Bat," concludes:

For something is amiss or out of place
When mice with wings can wear a human face.

It took time for Roethke to learn how full the world is of such appari-tions . . . and worse!

The confirmation that he was in full possession of his art and of his vision came seven years later, with the publication of *The Lost Son* (1948), whose opening sequence of "greenhouse poems" recaptures a significant portion of his inheritance. Roethke was born, of Teutonic stock, in Saginaw, Michigan, in 1908. The world of his childhood was a world of spacious commercial greenhouses, the capital of his florist father's dominion. Greenhouse: "my symbol for the whole of life, a womb, a heaven-on-earth," was Roethke's revealing later gloss. In its moist fecundity, its rank sweats and enclosure, the greenhouse certainly suggests a womb, an inexhaustible mother. If it stands as well for a heaven-on-earth, it is a strange kind of heaven, with its scums and mildews and smuts, its lewd monkey-tail roots, its snaky shoots. The boy of the poems is both fascinated and repelled by the avidity of the life-principle, by the bulbs that break out of boxes "hunting for chinks in the dark." He himself endures the agony of birth, with "this urge, wrestle, resurrection of dry sticks, cut stems struggling to put down feet." "What saint," he asks, "strained so much, rose on such lopped limbs to a new life?" This transparent womb is a place of adventures, fears, temptations, where the orchids are "so many devouring infants!":

> They lean over the path,
> Adder-mouthed,
> Swaying close to the face,
> Coming out, soft and deceptive,
> Limp and damp, delicate as a young bird's tongue.

When he goes out to the swampland to gather moss for lining cemetery baskets, he learns of the sin committed *contra naturam,* the desecration against the whole scheme of life, as if he had "disturbed some rhythm, old and of vast importance, by pulling off flesh from the living planet"—his own flesh. And he encounters death in a thousand rotting faces—all of them his own—as at the mouldy hecatomb he contemplates death crowning death, in a dump of vegetation . . . "over the dying, the newly dead."

The poet's green, rich world of childhood was self-contained, complete in itself. Mother waited there: she was all flowering. When father entered, that principle of authority, he was announced by pipe-knock and the cry, "Ordnung! Ordnung!" So much wilderness! and all of it under glass, organized, controlled. For the rest of his life Roethke was to seek a house for his spirit that would be as green, as various, as ordered. And he was often to despair of finding it. In one of his last poems, "Otto," named after his father, he concludes:

> The long pipes knocked: it was the end of night.
> I'd stand upon my bed, a sleepless child

Watching the waking of my father's world.—
O world so far away! O my lost world!

Roethke's passionate and near-microscopic scrutiny of the chemistry of
growth extended beyond "the lives on a leaf" to the world of what he termed
"the minimal," or "the lovely diminutives," the very least of creation, including "beetles in caves, newts, stone-deaf fishes, lice tethered to long limp
subterranean weeds, squirmers in bogs, and bacterial creepers." These are
creatures still wet with the waters of the beginning. At or below the threshold
of the visible they correspond to that darting, multitudinous life of the mind
under the floor of the rational, in the wet of the subconscious.

Roethke's immersion in these waters led to his most heroic enterprise, the
sequence of interior monologues which he initiated with the title poem of
The Lost Son, which he continued in *Praise to the End!* (1951), and which
he persisted up to the last in returning to, through a variety of modifications
and developments. "Each poem," he once wrote, "is complete in itself; yet
each in a sense is a stage in a kind of struggle out of the slime; part of a slow
spiritual progress; an effort to be born, and later, to become something
more." The method is associational rather than logical, with frequent time
shifts in and out of childhood, in and out of primitive states of consciousness
and even the synesthesia of infancy. Motifs are introduced as in music, with
the themes often developing contrapuntally. Rhythmically he was after "the
spring and rush of the child," he said . . . "and Gammer Gurton's concision:
mutterkin's wisdom." There are throwbacks to the literature of the folk, to
counting rhymes and play songs, to Mother Goose, to the songs and rants of
Elizabethan and Jacobean literature, to the Old Testament, the visions of
Blake and the rhapsodies of Christopher Smart. But the poems, original and
incomparable, belong to the poet and not to his sources.

The protagonist, who recurrently undertakes the dark journey into his own
underworld, is engaged in a quest for spiritual identity. The quest is
simultaneously a flight, for he is being pursued by the man he has become,
implacable, lost, soiled, confused. In order to find himself he must lose himself by reexperiencing all the stages of his growth, by reenacting all the
transmutations of his being from seed-time to maturity. We must remember
that it is the poet himself who plays all the parts. He is Proteus and all the
forms of Proteus—flower, fish, reptile, amphibian, bird, dog, etc.—and he is
the adversary who hides among the rocks to pounce on Proteus, never letting
go his hold, while the old man of the sea writhes through his many shapes
until, exhausted by the struggle, he consents to prophesy in the *claritas* of his
found identity.

Curiously enough—for I am sure it was not a conscious application—
Roethke recapitulated the distinctive elements of this Protean imagery in a

prose commentary that appeared in 1950. "Some of these pieces," he wrote in *Mid-Century American Poets,* referring to his sequence of monologues, "Begin in the mire; as if man is no more than a shape writhing from the old rock." His annotation of a line of his from *Praise to the End!*—"I've crawled from the mire, alert as a saint or a dog"—reads: "Except for the saint, everything else is dog, fish, minnow, bird, etc., and the euphoric ride resolves itself into a death-wish."

Roethke's explanation of his "cyclic" method of narration, a method that depends on periodic recessions of the movement instead of advances in a straight line, seems to me particularly noteworthy. "I believe," he wrote, "that to go forward as a spiritual man it is necessary first to go back. Any history of the psyche (or allegorical journey) is bound to be a succession of experiences, similar yet dissimilar. There is a perpetual slipping-back, then a going forward; but there is *some* 'progress'."

This comment can be linked with several others by Roethke that I have already quoted: references to "the struggle out of the slime," the beginning "in the mire." I think also of his unforgettably defiant affirmation: "In spite of all the muck and welter, the dark, the *dreck* of these poems, I count myself among the happy poets."

In combination these passages point straight to the door of Dr. Jung or to the door of Jung's disciple Maud Bodkin, whose *Archetypal Patterns in Poetry* was familiar to Roethke. In Jung's discussion of Progression and Regression as fundamental concepts of the Libido-theory in his *Contributions to Analytical Psychology,* he describes progression as "the daily advance of the process of psychological adaptation," which at certain times fails. Then "the vital feeling" disappears; there is a damming-up of energy, of libido. At such times neurotic symptoms are observed, and repressed contents appear, of interior and unadapted character. "Slime out of the depths," he calls such contents—but slime that contains not only "objectionable animal tendencies, but also germs of new possibilities of life." Before "a renewal of life" can come about, there must be an acceptance of the possibilities that lie in the unconscious contents of the mind "activated through regression . . . and disfigured by the slime of the deep."

This principle is reflected in the myth of "the night journey under the sea," as in the Book of Jonah, or in the voyage of The Ancient Mariner, and is related to dozens of myths, in the rebirth archetype, that tell of the descent of the hero into the underworld and of his eventual return back to the light. The monologues of Roethke follow the pattern of progression and regression and belong unmistakably to the rebirth archetype.

In the opening section of "The Lost Son," for example, the hallucinated protagonist, regressing metamorphically, sinks down to an animistic level, begging from the sub-human some clue as to the meaning of his existence:

>   At Woodlawn I heard the dead cry:
>   I was lulled by the slamming of iron,
>   A slow drip over stones,
>   Toads brooding wells.
>   All the leaves stuck out their tongues;
>   I shook the softening chalk of my bones,
>   Saying,
>   Snail, snail, glister me forward,
>   Bird, soft-sigh me home.
>   Worm, be with me.
>   This is my hard time.

At the close of the same poem, which remains for me the finest of the monologues, the protagonist, turned human and adult again, is granted his moment of epiphany; but he is not ready yet to apprehend it wholly; he must wait:

>   It was beginning winter,
>   The light moved slowly over the frozen field,
>   Over the dry seed-crowns,
>   The beautiful surviving bones
>   Swinging in the wind.
>
>   Light traveled over the field;
>   Stayed.
>   The weeds stopped swinging.
>   The mind moved, not alone,
>   Through the clear air, in the silence.
>
>   Was it light?
>   Was it light within?
>   Was it light within light?
>   Stillness becoming alive,
>   Yet still?
>
>   A lively understandable spirit
>   Once entertained you.
>   It will come again.
>   Be still.
>   Wait.

The love poems that followed early in the 1950's—Roethke was forty-four when he married—were a distinct departure from the painful excavations of the monologues and in some respects a return to the strict stanzaic forms of his earliest work. They were daring and buoyant, not only in their explicit sensuality, their "lewd music," but in the poet's open and arrogant usurpation of the Yeatsian beat and, to a degree, of the Yeatsian mantle:

> I take this cadence from a man named Yeats;
> I take it, and I give it back again. . . .

By this time Roethke had the authority, the self-assurance, indeed the euphoria—"I am most immoderately married"—to carry it off.

Even when he had been involved with the *dreck* of the monologues, he was able, in sudden ecstatic seizures of clarity, to proclaim "a condition of joy." Moreover, he had been delighted at the opportunity that the free and open form gave him to introduce juicy little bits of humor, mostly puns and mangled bawdry and indelicate innuendoes. He had also written some rather ferocious nonsense verse for children. Now he achieved something much more difficult and marvelous: a passionate love poetry that yet included the comic, as in "I Knew a Woman," with its dazzling first stanza:

> I knew a woman, lovely in her bones,
> When small birds sighed, she would sigh back at them;
> Ah, when she moved, she moved more ways than one:
> The shapes a bright container can contain!
> Of her choice virtues only gods should speak,
> Or English poets who grew up on Greek
> (I'd have them sing in chorus, cheek to cheek).

Inevitably the beloved is a shapeshifter, like the poet himself. "Slow, slow as a fish she came." Or again, "She came toward me in the flowing air, a shape of change." "No mineral man," he praises her as dove, as lily, as rose, as leaf, even as "the oyster's weeping foot." And he asks himself, half fearfully: "Is she what I become? Is this my final Face?"

At the human level this tendency of his to become the other is an extension of that Negative Capability, as defined by Keats, which first manifested itself in the Roethke greenhouse. A man of this nature, said Keats, "is capable of being in uncertainties, mysteries, doubt, without any irritable reaching after fact and reason . . . he has no identity—he is continually in for and filling some other body." In "The Dying Man" Roethke assumes the character of the poet Yeats; in "Meditations of an Old Woman," he writes as though he were his mother; in several late poems he adopts the role and voice of his beloved.

The love poems gradually dissolve into the death poems. Could the flesh be transcended, as he had at first supposed, till passion burned with a spiritual light? Could his several selves perish in love's fire and be reborn as one? Could the dear and beautiful one lead him, as Dante taught, to the very footstool of God? In "The Dying Man" he proposes a dark answer: "All sensual love's but dancing on the grave." Roethke thought of himself as one with the dying Yeats: "I am that final thing, a man learning to sing."

The five-fold "Meditations of an Old Woman" that concludes Roethke's selective volume, *Words for the Wind* (1958), is almost wholly preoccupied with thoughts of death and with the search for God. He had started writing the sequence almost immediately after the death of his mother in 1955. Here he returns to the cyclic method of the earlier monologues. In the first Meditation the Old Woman introduces the theme of journeying. All journeys, she reflects, are the same, a movement forward after a few wavers, and then a slipping backward, "backward in time." Once more we recognize the Jungian pattern of progression and regression embodied in the work. The journeys and the five meditations as a whole are conceived in a kind of rocking motion, and indeed the verb "to rock"—consistently one of the poet's key verbs of motion—figures prominently in the text. The rocking is from the cradle toward death:

> The body, delighting in thresholds,
> Rocks in and out of itself. . . .

An image of transformations. And toward the close:

> To try to become like God
> Is far from becoming God.
> O, but I seek and care!
>
> I rock in my own dark,
> Thinking, God has need of me.
> The dead love the unborn.

A few weeks before his death Roethke completed his arrangement of some fifty new poems, published last July under the title, *The Far Field*. The range and power of this posthumous volume, unquestionably one of the landmarks of the American imagination, have yet to be fully grasped or interpreted. Among its contents are two major sequences, "The North American Sequence," consisting of six long meditations on the American landscape and on death . . . on dying into America, so to speak; and a group of twelve shorter, more formal lyrics, under the generic heading, "Sequence, Sometimes Metaphysical," bearing witness to a state of spiritual crisis, the dance of the soul around the exhausted flesh and toward the divine fire.

"How to transcend this spiritual emptiness?" he cries in "The Longing," which opens the "North American Sequence." The self, retracing its transformations, seeks refuge in a lower order of being:

> And the spirit fails to move forward,
> But shrinks into a half-life, less than itself,
> Falls back, a slug, a loose worm
> Ready for any crevice,
> An eyeless starer.

He longs "for the imperishable quiet at the heart of form."

In a sense he has completed his dark journey, but he has not yet found either his oblivion or his immortality. He yearns for the past which will also be future. The American earth calls to him, and he responds by struggling out of his lethargy: "I am coming!" he seems to be saying, "but wait a minute. I have something left to do. I belong to the wilderness. I will yet speak in tongues."

> I have left the body of the whale, but the mouth of the night
>   is still wide;
> On the Bullhead, in the Dakotas, where the eagles eat well,
> In the country of few lakes, in the tall buffalo grass
>   at the base of the clay buttes,
> In the summer heat, I can smell the dead buffalo,
> The stench of their damp fur drying in the sun,
> The buffalo chips drying.

> Old men should be explorers?
> I'll be an Indian.
> Ogalala?
> Iroquois.

That diminishing coda is a miracle of compression and connotation.

In "The Far Field," the fifth poem of the "North American Sequence" and the title poem of the collection, Roethke speaks of his journeying, as his mother did in the earlier Meditations:

> I dream of journeys repeatedly:
> Of flying like a bat deep into a narrowing tunnel,
> Of driving alone, without luggage, out a long peninsula,
> The road lined with snow-laden second growth,
> A fine dry snow ticking the windshield,
> Alternate snow and sleet, no on-coming traffic,
> And no lights behind, in the blurred side-mirror,
> The road changing from glazed tarface to a rubble of stone,
> Ending at last in a hopeless sand-rut,
> Where the car stalls,
> Churning in a snowdrift
> Until the headlights darken.

As always, in these soliloquies, the poet sinks through various levels of time and of existence. There was a field once where he found death in the shape of a rat, along with other creatures shot by the nightwatchman or mutilated by the mower; but he found life, too, in the spontaneous agitations of the birds, "a twittering restless cloud." And he tries to relive his selfhood back to its mindless source, so that he may be born again, meanwhile proclaiming his faith in the inexorable wheel of metamorphosis:

> I'll return again,
> As a snake or a raucous bird,
> Or, with luck, as a lion.

Sometimes the faith wavers. In "The Abyss," a poem outside the "North American Sequence," he inquires, "Do we move toward God, or merely another condition?" . . . "I rock between dark and dark."

An even deeper anguish saturates the verses of the "Sequence, Sometimes Metaphysical:"

> Dark, dark my light, and darker my desire.
> My soul, like some heat-maddened summer fly,
> Keeps buzzing at the sill. Which I is *I*?

But if the shapeshifter for a moment despairs of his identity, he still has strength and will enough to drag himself over the threshold of annihilation.

> A fallen man, I climb out of my fear.
> The mind enters itself, and God the mind,
> And one is One, free in the tearing wind.

I do not always believe in these ecstatic resolutions—they sometimes seem a cry of need rather than of revelation—but I am always moved by the presence of the need and by the desperation of the voice.

"Brooding on God, I may become a man," writes Roethke in "The Marrow," out of the same sequence—one of the great poems of the century, a poem at once dreadful and profound, electric and shuddering:

> Godhead above my God, are you there still?
> To sleep is all my life. In sleep's half-death,
> My body alters, altering the soul
> That once could melt the dark with its small breath.
> Lord, hear me out, and hear me out this day:
> From me to Thee's a long and terrible way.

> I was flung back from suffering and love
> When light divided on a storm-tossed tree.
> Yea, I have slain my will, and still I live;
> I would be near; I shut my eyes to see;
> I bleed my bones, their marrow to bestow
> Upon that God who knows what I would know.

Such furious intensity exacts a price. The selves of the poet could be fused only by the exertion of a tremendous pressure. If only he could be content to name the objects that he loved and not be driven to convert them into symbols—that painful ritual.

In "The Far Field," where he evokes his own valedictory image, Whitman is with him, and Prospero, and—in the shifting light—Proteus, the old man of the sea, fatigued by his changes:

> An old man with his feet before the fire,
> In robes of green, in garments of adieu.

The lines that follow have a touch of prophecy in them as the poet, renewed by the thought of death, leaving his skins behind him, moves out into the life-giving and obliterating waters:

> A man faced with his own immensity
> Wakes all the waves, all their loose wandering fire.
> The murmur of the absolute, the why
> Of being born fails on his naked ears.
> His spirit moves like monumental wind
> That gentles on a sunny blue plateau.
> He is the end of things, the final man.
>
> All finite things reveal infinitude:
> The mountain with its singular bright shade
> Like the blue shine on freshly frozen snow,
> The after-light upon ice-burdened pines;
> Odor of basswood on a mountain-slope,
> A scent beloved of bees;
> Silence of water above a sunken tree:
> The pure serene of memory in one man,—
> A ripple widening from a single stone
> Winding around the waters of the world.

James McMichael

The Poetry of Theodore Roethke

In the last section of his North American Sequence, Theodore Roethke defines a concern that is dominant in all his poetry.

> Near this rose, in this grove of sun-parched, wind-warped madronas,
> Among the half-dead trees, I came upon the true ease of myself,
> As if another man appeared out of the depths of my being,
> And I stood outside myself,
> Beyond becoming and perishing,
> A something wholly other.

From his first book, *Open House,* through his last, *The Far Field,* Roethke's poems persistently realize his need to be "A something wholly other." The experience is one that he describes as "the journey out of the self." There is a temptation to discuss each of his books of poetry as a separate segment of that journey, but I find it much more accurate to describe them as rehearsals, in wildly differing forms, of the same journey. However long the journey may be—and I suggest that it was neither shorter nor longer than his own life—it is too simple to admit distinct stages. The journey is as simple as moving from one point, which is circumscribed by his sense of having an identity that is limited in time and space, to another in which those limitations no longer seem real. I want to define both what motivates Roethke to attempt this journey, and the attempts themselves.

Although the poems of *Open House* are the least representative and the weakest, we can see in several of them the earliest instances of Roethke's journey out of the self. "The Auction" is probably the most obvious in this respect. The speaker of the poem describes his own "pride," "illusion" and "fear"—internal characteristics, and possibly those most responsible for making the self an unhappy place—as being miraculously external to him and up for auction. Although they had been his "choice possessions," he found, to his subsequent pleasure, that he "did not move to claim what was [his] own." He leaves the auction "with unencumbered will/ And all the rubbish of confusion sold." The tone of these, the last lines of the poem, is rigidly cheery and resembles not at all what we are to find in the poems of his later books. He is struggling to believe that the self has been purged of all its

From *The Southern Review,* V (Winter 1969), 4-25. Reprinted by permission of the author and *The Southern Review.*

unhealthy elements; that the journey out of the self, insofar as it was necessary to do so, has been completed. When we consider it in the context of his subsequent poetry we can see how extremely strained the rhetoric of this poem is. In fact, the tone of *Open House* as a whole might best be described as a kind of strained restraint. Although the highly regular and tightly end-stopped iambic lines are characteristic of individual poems from later books, the proportion of poems in traditional meters to those in free verse is overwhelmingly greater in *Open House*. With the looser rhythms in the later books will come the admission that all is not well in the self.

If we turn to a late poem, "The Marrow," I think we will begin to see why the self is something that he wants very intensely to leave. In the third of the four stanzas the speaker addresses God directly, first asking the "Godhead above [his] God" if He is "there still," and pleading with the deity to acknowledge his plight: "Lord, hear me out, and hear me out this day:/ From me to Thee's a long and terrible way." It is the separation between himself and the ultimate divinity that has aroused in him the "Desire, desire, desire" that concludes the second stanza. This separation and the desire to eliminate it are respectively the subject matter and tone of Roethke's most serious poems. It is his awareness of his identity, his awareness of self, that reminds him almost obsessively that he is distinct from everything beyond the limits of that identity.

But to know more precisely what Roethke has experienced, we need to formulate a clearer understanding of the nature of the Godhead above his God. Roethke does not define the nature of his deity for us. Were he able to do so, his sense of separation from it would be the less intense. To say this is not to say, however, that God is not immanent for him. In "A Walk in Late Summer" from *Words for the Wind* he describes his own existence as being contingent upon God's immanence. "God's in that stone, or I am not a man!" Still, what we learn about his deity must be recovered by examining the dynamics of his relationship to it as they are are manifested in the conflict between self and soul. It is the soul's business to "know" God in the most intimate way—to be at one with Him. But there is nothing for the "soul to understand" except "the slack face of the dismal pure inane." Were the soul free of the self, the intuitive kind of knowing that is characteristic of communion with the deity might be realized. For the self demands that knowledge take place on the terms that it lays down: whatever is known must conform to the requirement that it be intellectually—not intuitively—apprehensible. Whatever does not conform must necessarily remain, for the self, inane. In trying to complete the journey out of the self, "It lies upon us to undo the lie/ Of living merely in the realm of time." And yet the conceptual capacity that is definitive of the self makes it impossible to be unaware of our temporal limitations.

It is important to remember, though, that the journey out of the self is a spatial metaphor. The soul is only able to do its proper work when it is enough liberated from self to participate immediately with something external to the self. Roethke speaks very explicitly about this task in a late essay, "On 'Identity' ":

> To look at a thing so long that you are a part of it and it is a part of you. If you can effect this, then you are by way of getting somewhere: knowing you will break from self-involvement, from I to Otherwise, or maybe even to Thee. The sense that all is one and one is all. This is inevitably accompanied by a loss of the "I," the purely human ego, to another center, a sense of the absurdity of death, a return to a state of innocency. This experience has come to me so many times, in so many varying circumstances, that I cannot suspect its validity. . . .

It is precisely this kind of experience that he is defining in "A Walk in Late Summer." He watches the "soft-backed creatures" as they cross his lawn, and he tells us that he "would know their ways." "The small! The small! I hear them singing clear/ On the long banks, in the soft summer air." To know the ways of the small is, in the self's terms, to know nothing. It is to encounter contingency without sensing a separation from it; to encounter it without fearing that implicit in its change, and in your own, is the spectre of death.

To know the ways of the small is also to know what Roethke describes in "The Swan" as "that nothing from which all is made." The clearest way that I know to define how this notion relates to Roethke's self, soul and deity is to introduce as a gloss a brief section from Pascal's *Pensées*. In doing so I am not interested in making a case that it is a source for Roethke, and the reader will have to decide for himself whether Pascal's notions are really or only incidentally relevant to those of Roethke.

According to Pascal, the universe is so vast that no idea can approach it; in trying to imagine its vastness, man is led to think of himself as a nothing in comparison to the all. But what he is tempted to overlook is the fact that he is by his nature as distantly removed from the smallest part of the universe as he is from the largest. Let any man exhaust all his powers in trying to find the smallest thing in nature, a thing as absolute in its simplicity as infinity is in its complexity. When that man is confident that he has found it, Pascal says, "I will make him see within it a new abyss. In the enclosure of that abridged atom I will describe not only the visible universe, but all the immensity that can be conceived in nature." For no matter how simple a thing man attempts to know, no matter how intensely he gives himself to the kind of intuition that might convince him that he is at one with that simple thing, his ability to conceptualize is so integral to him that he will be forced to recognize in it the qualities that it shares with infinity.

And so man is "equally incapable of seeing the nothing from which he is made, and the infinity in which he is engulfed." Could he suspend his intelligence, the nothing from which all is made might be available to him. But man can know neither extreme: the nothing and the all are both infinitely inaccessible to him. "It is as if extreme things do not exist for us. This is our true condition; it is this that makes us incapable of certain knowledge and absolute ignorance." Unlike all the other parts of the creation—the beasts and inanimate nature—man is both mind and body; and it is his dual nature that comprises his isolation from God's immanence. The extremities of the nothing and the all "meet and reunite by force of distance, and find each other in God, and only in God."

As they relate to Roethke's poetry, the relevance of Pascal's remarks is this: they suggest that the mindless simplicity which tends toward the extreme of nothing is as viable a road to God as the more mindful one. Although it entails choosing the best of the two possible routes, it is a belief resembling Pascal's that enables Roethke to direct the journey out of the self toward the small rather than the big. "I believe that to go forward as a spiritual man," Roethke has told us, "it is necessary first to go back." The intelligence is not, for him, the avenue to God. Instead, it obstructs his immediate participation with God's immanence as it is manifested in the world outside himself. Because his mind provides him with the ability to abstract himself from whatever he meets "beyond [his] outer skin," he is irrevocably separate, as long as he is alive, from the simplicity of God's creation. He may "Sing of that nothing from which all is made," but the mind will insist on working, reminding him perpetually that he is a self. What he sees outside himself may remind him no less that he is a soul: "Hello, thingy spirit," he exclaims in a poem from "The Lost Son" sequence. But the mindlessness required of him, if he is to be purely a soul and at one with his God, is something that he can only "desire, desire, desire." It is out of this desire that his poems are built. They are definitions—all of them—of a creation that mediates between self and God. His soul "knows" the creation to be mindless and inane, and it "knows" well enough that God is neither. But it can affirm the creation and God's immanence only on the terms that it shares with the simplicity of "the small": and those terms are mindless.

"The Beast" is perhaps as explicit a definition of his quest for mindlessness as Roethke has given us.

> I came to a great door,
> Its lintel overhung
> With burr, bramble, and thorn;
> And when it swung, I saw
> A meadow, lush and green.

> And there a great beast played,
> A sportive, aimless one,
> A shred of bone its horn,
> And colloped round with fern.
> It looked at me; it stared.
>
> Swaying, I took its gaze;
> Faltered; rose up again;
> Rose but to lurch and fall,
> Hard, on the gritty sill,
> I lay; I languished there.
>
> When I raised myself once more,
> The great round eyes had gone.
> The long lush grass lay still;
> And I wept there, alone.

With no more information than the poem itself provides, it is tenuous to posit the mind as the source of the faltering, lurching, and falling to which he refers in the third stanza. And yet it is clearly as "A sportive, aimless one" that the beast is attractive to him. The primitive simplicity that comes with the repetition of the pronoun in the line "It looked at me; it stared" is reinforced throughout the poem in the rather stiff and at times almost awkward trimeter. Although the poem scans as being traditionally metrical, its rhythms are considerably more energetic than all but a few of those we find in *Open House*. In the context of the present poem, what this energy implies, it seems to me, is his elemental need to believe that he is not separate from the creation he sees outside himself. It is a need for mediators who are at once other than himself and unmistakably more real than his ideas of them.

In the first stanza of the first of the eight poems comprising "The Lost Son" sequence, Roethke makes an invocation to the animate but subhuman mediators.

> Snail, snail, glister me forward,
> Bird, soft-sigh me home,
> Worm, be with me.
> This is my hard time.

Roethke has spoken of the poem, telling us that its protagonist is "so geared-up, so over-alive that he is hunting, like a primitive, for some animistic suggestion, some clue to existence from the sub-human." Each poem in the sequence sustains this frenetic quality, and each refers to new animals until the list itself is overwhelming: spider, moth, eel, sheep, rat, mouse, cat, otter, mole, fish, dog, snake, cow, lark, kitten, horse, hen, goose, goat, mare, kill-deer, lizard, bee, toad, she-bear, silver fish, mollusk, frog, wasp, minnow, heron, crab, flicker, fly, owl, heifer, hog, sparrow, winter-wasp, beetle, pigeon, hedge wren, bat, dolphin. The sequence as a whole is essentially about going back. As he describes it in another poem, "I knew I had been there before,/ In that cold, granitic slime." It is the animal world that mediates between himself and the soil. "Who stunned the dirt into noise?/ Ask the mole, he knows."

But if the sequence is primarily about going back, about directing the journey out of the self toward the smallest and simplest parts of God's creation, so too does it introduce us to the protagonist's own biological impulses which lead him to woman, that complex creature. "For whom have I swelled like a seed?/ What a bone ache I have." Of all the mediators on his journey out of the self, the woman is the most easily invoked. Like him, she is distinct from subhuman creation because she has a mind; and yet it is precisely that her body differs from his that he is attracted to her. She is beguilingly other, and as such Roethke conceives of and responds to her as if she has intimate traffic with the subhuman and inanimate otherness, and her presence is felt in poems in which she does not explicitly appear. For example, in "A Light Breather" there is no reference to her: it is a poem about the spirit as it communes with the external world. But the sexual implications of the poem's diction and movement are unmistakable, and she is very subtly evoked. She makes an appearance in "The Visitant," and again she shares an intimacy with the natural world. Before she pays her visit, the poet hears a voice that instructs him to "Stay by the slip-ooze." And shortly:

> Slow, slow as a fish she came,
> Slow as a fish coming forward,
> Swaying in a long wave;
> Her skirts not touching a leaf,
> Her white arms reaching towards me.

Throughout *The Collected Poems* she is characterized as being closer to the soil than her lover, and it implied that her value is accordingly the greater.

Present in all of Roethke's love poems is his belief that sexual desire and its ultimate fulfillment are central to his moving beyond the limits of self. Here is the last stanza from "Words for the Wind."

> I kiss her moving mouth,
> Her swart hilarious skin;
> She breaks my breath in half;
> She frolicks like a beast;
> And I dance round and round,
> A fond and foolish man,
> And see and suffer myself
> In another being, at last.

Each of the love poems contains a line that refers to sexual intercourse in detail that is varyingly graphic from poem to poem. The rhetorical burden of these lines, clearly, is to evoke the desirability of his lover. The references are frequently to the way she moves. "Ah, when she moved, she moved more ways than one." "She moved in circles, and those circles moved." "She moves as water moves, and comes to me,/ Stayed by what was, and pulled by what would be." The best of the love poems, "Four for Sir John Davies," is organized around explicit references to the sexual intimacies of the poet and his "partner." The repetitive structure of the poem emphasizes the basic simplicity of the act upon which the more complicated argument of the poem is built. The first section establishes his need for the partner, but not until the second section in which "She kissed [him] close, and then did something else" is she represented as being physically there. For the rest of the poem, however, she is as close to him as she can be. "She laughed me out, and then she laughed me in;/ In the deep middle of ourselves we lay" he tells us in the third section; and then in the last, "The links were soft between us; still, we kissed;/ We undid chaos to a curious sound."

To this point in the essay I have emphasized that the *sine qua non* of Roethke's journey out of the self is his commitment to the mindless part of God's creation, and I have done so because the rhetoric of his poems consistently underscores this commitment. He desires to be at one with what he experiences as the world outside the self: being at one with it would be to forget his smallness and perishability in the context of the universe. But it is no less true that, rhetoric or no rhetoric, such forgetting is impossible. The qualifications I am about to make should in no way be interpreted as contradicting my description of the journey as one that is essentially simple. The journey clearly involves his accepting something other than himself on its own terms, of loving it for what it is. The more he thinks about that thing, the less likely he is to know it as it really is; for as soon as it begins to acquire for him any of the qualities that his conceptual faculty is ready to impose upon it, his intuition and love of it are lost. The love poems stress that his simple biological attraction for women, both because it is mindless and because she seems to him more mindless than himself, is the most natural and most necessary first step on the journey.

But however basic to his love he conceives the sexual act to be, he knows that he is not mindless. His need to live beyond his outer skin in the body of his lover may make him "dancing-mad," as he tells us in "Four for Sir John Davies"; but it is Yeats, as well as the bears, who knows how that came to be. The dance itself is very literally doing "what the clumsy partner wants to do," but it has figurative implications that extend temporally to Sir John Davies and Dante, and that extend spatially throughout the universe as a whole. He desires as energetically that his dance guarantee him immortality as he does that it absorb him in an act that is mindlessly affirmative of the creation. What Dante, Davies, Yeats, and Roethke know is that "The word outleaps the world, and light is all." The latter two have found themselves and language "In that dark world where gods have lost their way." It has been only by virtue of their desire to restore both the light and the divinity that their art, a verbal one, has acquired a value that is not inherent in the world. To understand more particularly what this value is, we must consider the role of the word in the very different world in which Dante and Davies lived.

Man's belief about his role in the universe has changed radically from the one represented in Davies' long poem *Orchestra.* For Davies, as for most of the poets who wrote before the impact of seventeenth-century new science, the divine light and love had created out of chaos a universe so ordered that each of man's experiences was inherently meaningful. These men lived in a universe "instinct with meaning," as Rosemond Tuve has described it, and because they did the words they used in talking about it had the kind of value that they can have only with the support of an ontology which attributes as much reality to universals as it does to particulars. For Dante and for Davies, the "word outleaps the world" in the sense that their experience is more real according to the order they are permitted to apprehend in it—and their tool in this activity is the universal, the concept, the word.

Now "Four for Sir John Davies" is not a poem about the decay of language in the modern world. Although Roethke tells us that his "blood leaped with a wordless song," he doesn't seem to be more than incidentally interested in what words can and cannot do. But as a poet, the question of their value is necessarily relevant to him. It becomes even more so in a poem such as this one in which he describes his world as one without an inherent order that is intelligible. Since he cannot believe that such harmony obtains in his world, neither can he believe in the reality of universals. The words are there to be used, just as they had been for Davies. Out of them he might construct a world no less tightly ordered, no less meaningful than Davies' own. But such a construction would necessarily be weak. Indeed, it is precisely his word-making capacity that frustrates him. His concepts are simultaneously formed of and imposed upon the external world with which he wants to atone. Because his concepts of that world cannot be identical with it—the former being general and static, the latter particular and transient—his absolute separation from the external world is assured. Whatever he builds out of language must be grounded, as firmly as possible, in something outside himself. As we have seen, this thing is the particular and transient moment during sexual intercourse in which he participates as immediately and intuitively as he can with that creature outside himself with whom he is in love. It is through his body, not his mind, that he moves from self to soul: "The body and the soul know how to play/ In that dark world where gods have lost their way." "The flesh can make the spirit visible."

And yet in the final couplet he insists that there is an important distinction between body and soul: "Who rise from flesh to spirit know the fall:/ The word outleaps the world, and light is all." To experience his partner as intuitively as he can is to give himself totally to the flesh, to be totally of the "dark world" that the word ultimately exceeds. In his union with her he is in fact so much of "that dark world" that he "gave her kisses back, and woke a ghost." Roethke would seem to be at least tangentially alluding here to the Elizabethan association of sexual intercourse and death. But the connotations of the activity itself are entirely positive; for Roethke suggests that the "death" they experience through their union is proof of their immortality. The process of giving the self is miraculously, almost spiritually transforming. In the third section of the poem, entitled "The Wraith," he asks "What shape leaped forward at the sensual cry?—/ Sea-beast or bird . . .?" He can answer only that "It was and was not she, a shape alone,/ Impaled on light . . ." It is in having "dared the dark" by engaging one another as the other really is that they "reach the white and warm." The transformation that follows is "the rise from flesh to spirit" and the momentary restoration of a value that "outleaps the world" and illuminates infinity.

 "Four for Sir John Davies" is one of the most comprehensive of Roethke's shorter poems in that it is representative of his simultaneous desire for the nothing and the all. In taking the cadence from Yeats and giving it back again he seems to imply that the poem itself might insure the preservation of his identity no less than would the progeny that might have been conceived during the sexual act which occasioned the poem. But however much the poem involves us in Roethke's desire for the universal and the permanent, we must not overlook the fact that the only satisfaction of that desire involves his proceeding through an experience that is singular and evanescent.

Because she is so desirable, Roethke has relatively little difficulty accepting and knowing his lover as she really is. Not until his last book, however, does he assume her own voice and imply thereby an even more intimate knowledge of her otherness. The role of his lover in *The Far Field* is a curious one, however. Her absence in his finest poem, "North American Sequence," is almost obtrusive. The sequence is his most complete definition of the journey out of the self: he constructs a hierarchy of mediators to help him in his need to realize his soul, but the woman is not one of these. To judge from the love poems in *The Far Field,* it seems as if his lover has brought him close enough to the external world that he can now concentrate his energy on defining that world rather than his relationship with her, as he had tended to do earlier. As he characterizes and speaks through her, she seems even more integrally atoned with natural phenomena. In "Her Longing," she speaks of herself as being "At one with the plants in the pond" until her desire to move beyond the limits of self becomes so great that "The wild stream, the sea itself cannot contain" her. But even in her transcendence as "a phoenix, sure of [her] body,/ Perpetually rising out of" herself, her activity is represented as being in very close contact with natural detail—her "wings hovering over the shore-birds,/ Or beating against the black clouds of the storm,/ Protecting the sea-cliffs." Again, in "Her Time," she tells us that

> before
> The long surf of the storm booms
> Down on the near shore,
> When everything—birds, men, dogs—
> Runs to cover:
> I'm one to follow,
> To follow.

It is as if she has taken him back with her into that mindless world in which his god inheres.

"North American Sequence" is an index to the thoroughness with which Roethke atones with the world outside the self. Although the sequence is over five hundred lines long, it demands being discussed in detail. There are six poems in the sequence, and each contains from three to five sections. The first poem is "The Longing." The first section of this poem defines that "bleak time" in which the other has been so corrupted by the collective self of man that it can inspire no longing for it in the individual self. The spirit can advance only when it brings self to other, but in the presence of "Saliva dripping from warm microphones" and the "Agony of crucifixion on bar-stools," "The spirit fails to move forward" and "Falls back, a slug, a loose worm." It is precisely this kind of falling back, as we have seen, that is requisite to moving forward; and in the second section, the poet's longing for what is outside the self has developed to the point that he wants to share an identity with the bud and the worm. But there is a resistance to the soul's moving forward as long as the self insists on asserting its identity with "pride." Roethke longs for the "felicity" of "A body with the motion of a soul," and this is what he sees in the mindless other outside himself. If he is to be a body with the motion of a soul, he must somehow atone with the other. That other is, in Pascal's sense of the term, a nothing. Roethke tells us that "Out of these nothings/ —All beginnings come."

With the exception of the last four lines, Section 2 is written exclusively in a tightly end-stopped iambic pentameter. In the third section, he begins writing in a free verse that is much looser and more expansive than what we find in Section 1; and as he does so, he uses the subjunctive in defining his longing to be at one with the other. "I would with the fish," he begins, and with the "children dancing." Besides his lover, his father and the child are Roethke's only human mediators: the child serves in this capacity, it would seem, because his powers of conceptualizing are not yet fully developed. In the "bleak time" described in Section 1, "Happiness" is left only "to dogs and children." "I would be a stream" and "love the leaves," and be where "the dark can be forgotten." But to do so he will have to "unlearn the lingo of exasperation, all the distortions of malice and hatred." As long as he cannot unlearn these things, as long as the self reminds him that he dare not forget his limitations to the extent that he can delight "in the redolent disorder of this mortal life," "the mouth of the night is still wide" for him.

The first poem closes with a reference to the Dakotas, and it functions as an excellent transitional vehicle.

> In the country of few lakes, in the tall buffalo grass
>   at the base of the clay buttes,
> In the summer heat, I can smell the dead buffalo,
> The stench of their damp fur drying in the sun,
> The buffalo chips drying.

The dryness, heat, and stench reflect the bleak time of Section 1. They remind us once again of the difficulties that the soul encounters in trying to break away from self to other. But the detail in these lines also reflects something of the charm and beauty of the other when it is contrasted with the detail of Section 1. "Old men should be explorers?" he asks. His answer, in the form of a resolution to be an Indian, raises a second question—one that was not posed in the poem's first appearance in *The Far Field*. What kind of an Indian shall he be? An Ogalala of the plains? No. Rather an Iroquois of the lakes. The dryness, heat, and stench will be replaced in the second poem with qualities that speak much better for the external world.

The entire sequence is organized around the relative values that the poet attributes to the various elements comprising the other. In general, the value of each element decreases according to its similarity to the self. With the exception of the rose, Roethke's treatment of which I will consider later in some detail, a consistent and apprehensible hierarchy of the creation is developed. The self is on the bottom of the hierarchy, the soul or spirit on the top:

> Spirit
>   Light
>   Air (wind)
>   Water
>   Sea
>   Fresh-water
>   Earth
>   Vegetable world

                    Animals
                        Birds (air)
                        Sub-human vertebrates (water, earth)
                        Child, father (earth only)
                Self

Since the self must engage representatives of each category in order to realize the soul's potential, it follows that these representatives serve as mediators no less than does the woman of the love poems. Adopting the terminology of Martin Buber, Roethke has defined as one of the most principle virtues the breaking away "from self-involvement, from I to Otherwise, or maybe even to Thee." A media*tor* implies the personal "Thou-ness" that Roethke seeks. Insofar as he can experience the creation as some*one* helping him to find his deity, the more immanent that deity is for him.

The second poem in the sequence, "Meditation at Oyster River," concerns the self's encounter with water, an element that is roughly in the middle of the hierarchy. In the first section, the self observes but is noticeably distinct from the water. "I dabble my toes in the brackish foam sliding forward,/ Then retire to a rock higher up on the cliffside." The more intimately the self engages water, air, and light—those orders that lack the solidity of the self— the more immediately does it know that its own solidity will eventually dissolve. Were he mindless, were he able to atone totally with the other, he would experience in these fluctuous orders no threat to his identity. But he has retreated from the water, and Section 2 begins with the declaration that "The self persists." Before he can again engage the water, he must solicit the help of a sub-human mediator, and so he acknowledges that "Death's face rises afresh,/ Among the shy beasts." After he gives us a catalogue of the activities of deer, doe, snake, fly, and hummingbird, he tells us first that "With these I would be"—then, immediately, "And with water."

The last five lines of section 2 involve him very directly with a description of the power and persistence of the tides. Section 3 begins:

                In this hour,
                In this first heaven of knowing,
                The flesh takes on the pure poise of the spirit,
                Acquires, for a time, the sandpiper's insouciance,
                The hummingbird's surety, the kingfisher's cunning—
                I shift on my rock, and I think:

Presumably, he is still on the same rock to which he had retired earlier in the poem. On the solidity of the rock, the self is relatively secure. But the flesh is taking on "the pure poise of the spirit," and he thinks not of the security of the earth, but rather, first, of the "tiny rivulet" that will gather volume and force as it moves further and further from the limitations of the earth, and, second, to the breakup of the ice on the river—another incident of solidity giving way to flux. In the very brief fourth section, he tells us that "Water's my will, and my way."

> And the spirit runs, intermittently,
> In and out of the small waves,
> Runs with the intrepid shorebirds—
> How graceful the small before danger!

The self still persists, as in a way it must as long as he's alive, but the rhetoric of his descriptive detail shows him intensely ready to court on its own terms everything outside himself that threatens his identity.

The third poem, "Journey to the Interior," introduces us to the metaphor of the automobile, a metaphor that will be repeated in the fifth poem of the sequence. The automobile serves the self in a protective capacity as the poet continues "the long journey out of the self." Although no one whom I have read or talked to agrees with me on this point, the journey to the interior seems to me to be not identical with the journey out of the self, but, instead, directly antithetical to it. By moving in the car to the interior and away from the water, the self is cautious of its security. "Better to hug close, wary of rubble and falling stones." The darkest and most dangerous aspects of the journey out of the self are the most other, and the section ends with the road being "blocked at last by a fallen fir-tree,/ The thickets darkening,/ the ravines ugly." He knows that the ultimate destination of the self, regardless of its caution, is its own annihilation.

Section 2 is somewhat digressive in the sense that it describes the car's traversing of the landscape in greater detail than did the first. There is an important difference between the two, however. In Section 1, the premium was on safety: here, it is on abandon.

> The trick was to throw the car sideways and charge over the
>   hill, full of the throttle.
> Grinding up and over the narrow road, spitting and roaring.
> A chance? Perhaps. But the road was part of me, and its ditches,
> And the dust lay thick on my eyelids,—Who ever wore goggles?—
> Always a sharp turn to the left past a barn close to the roadside,
> To a scurry of small dogs and a shriek of children . . .

And yet even though his engagement of danger is so thoroughgoing that the road is part of himself, the journey is still one to the interior. The length of the lines describing his ride in the car expand with his enthusiasm, but with a

reference to "water running between weeds," he is reminded that he is indeed
on a "detour."

> And all flows past—
> The cemetery with two scrubby trees in the middle of the prairie,
> The dead snakes and muskrats, the turtles gasping in the rubble,
> The spikey purple bushes in the winding dry creek bed—
> The floating hawks, the jackrabbits, the grazing cattle—
> I am not moving but they are,
> And the sun comes out of a blue cloud over the Tetons,
> While, farther away, the heat-lightning flashes.

Unlike the dead, the subhuman and vegetable kingdoms, and all the rapidly
changing conditions of the atmosphere, he will maintain, as long as he is alive,
the intelligence to fear the final dissolution of his identity into the limitless
creation external to him. It is the journey to the exterior—the absolute journey out of the self that comes with death—that he fears. "I rehearse myself
for this:" he tells us in the final section of the poem, "The stand at the
stretch in the face of death."

> As a blind man, lifting a curtain, knows it is morning,
> I know this change:
> On one side of silence there is no smile. . . .

But with so intimate an awareness of the self's vulnerability in the face of the
other, his sense of self is quieted. When this occurs he experiences a kind of
identity with the birds, "The spirit of wrath becomes the spirit of blessing,/
And the dead begin from their dark to sing in [his] sleep."
In the first section of the fourth poem, "The Long Waters," the poet
reflects upon the journey to the interior: "I acknowledge my foolishness with
God,/ My desire for the peaks, the black ravines." Proudly, he had sought to
ascend to God from the heights and depths of the land, to go forward without having first gone back completely enough to purge the self's fear of those
elements that threaten it most. The third poem has recorded one of those
detours that the self renders inevitable. "Meditation at Oyster River" had
prepared the self for its encounter with the sea and with its own transformation into spirit. But the self knew well enough that unlike the spirit it could
not run "intermittently,/ In and out of the small waves." Aware of its
temporal and spatial limitations, the self sought friendlier ground. In "The
Long Waters," with at least one detour behind him, the poet returns to "A
country of bays and inlets, and small streams flowing seaward." The short
second section begins as another detour: he implores Mnetha, the protectress

in Blake's "Tiriel," to shield him from the fate implicit in the other. But he quickly recognizes that danger must be courted if the beauty of the creation is to be known, and that, until it is known, the desire to journey out of the self is inoperative. Section 3 is a catalogue of beautiful natural detail, and it concludes by telling us that he has come,

> Blessed by the lips of a low wind,
> To a rich desolation of wind and water,
> To a landlocked bay, where the salt water is freshened
> By small streams running down under fallen fir trees.

Section 4 describes it as "a vulnerable place," and in 5, "the sea wind wakes desire" and he becomes "another thing."

The fifth of the six poems in the sequence is "The Far Field." The first section describes another journey in an automobile, but this one is not to the interior. It is a "dream," Roethke tells us, "Of driving alone, without luggage, out a long peninsula,"

> Ending at last in a hopeless sand-rut,
> Where the car stalls,
> Churning in a snowdrift
> Until the headlights darken.

Its conclusion is even more final in its bleakness than the one of "Journey to the Interior." In the second section, he learns of the "eternal" "in the shrunken face of a dead rat," and he confesses that, though he suffered for the subhuman creatures whose mortality had caught up with them, his grief was "not excessive." "For to come upon warblers in early May/ Was to forget time and death." The paradox of those mindless things that are born, grow and die is that they are at once more transient and more permanent than the concepts with which we try to structure our responses to them: they are survived by our cognition of their passing, but we who do the ordering are in turn survived by and subsumed under the natural process of which they serve as representatives. He imagines himself lying "naked in sand,"

> In the silted shallows of a slow river,
> Fingering a shell,
> Thinking:
> Once I was something like this, mindless,
> Or perhaps with another mind, less peculiar.

To find one's mindless self in spring is not to grieve for the dead or for the tenuousness of one's own identity. It is rather to live in concert with God's presence.

> I learned not to fear infinity,
> The far field, the windy cliffs of forever,
> The dying of time in the white light of tomorrow,
> The wheel turning away from itself,
> The sprawl of the wave,
> The on-coming water.

With the self's fears restrained, he defines what is to this point in the poem his most intimate relationship with the water, concluding with the declaration that he is "renewed" by the thought of dying, and that what he loves "is near at hand,/ Always, in earth and air."

So much has the rhetoric of the entire sequence directed us toward Roethke's desire to be at one with and to love what is "near at hand" that we can forget his corresponding need for what is most distant from him. The final section of "The Far Field" reminds us that for Roethke, "All finite things reveal infinitude." The mind that is a hindrance to him in his attempts to identify with the small is the same mind that enables him to attribute value to them, to conceive in them the infinite presence of God. The hierarchy that he reads in creation has for him the virtue of being distinctly literal. Light is very literally less solid than air, air than water, and so on. But as the literal particles composing these elements proceed up the hierarchy further and further toward the undifferentiated condition of nothing, the hierarchy itself remains figurative and implies a mind at work. It is the paradox of Roethke's poetry, as it is that of many others, that he cannot desire without a mind that permits him to abstract himself from the immediate and conceive of something better, cannot satisfy the desire as long as the mind insists on doing its job. The final poem in "North American Sequence," "The Rose," is his most ambitious attempt to define the paradox and thus achieve as much resolution concerning it as he can expect.

The implications of the rose as Roethke uses it are in one sense almost contradictory to the hierarchy of elements that has been at work in the first five poems of the sequence. For although it is of the vegetable kingdom and is literally less evanescent and more earthbound than representatives of those categories further up the hierarchical scale, it assumes a place on that scale above even light. And yet the last poem of the sequence is as devoted to sustaining the literal accuracy of the hierarchy as it is to suggesting for the rose a figurative transcendence of it. Roethke begins the poem by telling us that the place "where sea and fresh water meet" is "important," and we must infer why this is so. Now streams traverse a visible landscape; lakes are completely surrounded by land: fresh water is thus more of the interior than is the sea. We have seen that for Roethke the land is an insufficient retreat for those afraid to abandon the self, an abandonment that is inevitable—in death. What is required of us when we decide the importance of the place where fresh water meets the sea is this: we must assume, with Roethke, that value is inherent in the categories themselves, and—what is actually the same thing—that their values relative to one another depend upon their literal differences. Given the intensity with which Roethke wants to identify with the water, the literal meeting of river and sea realizes the most complete abandonment of limitation that the element can undergo. Almost from line to line, *The Collected Poems* has about it a quality that I can only describe as disjunctive: its effect, in every instance, is to force us to make inferences that are informed (1) by what we know from our own experience about the natural objects to which Roethke constantly refers us, and (2) by his no less constant implication that God resides, with degrees of immanence that vary according to their literal composition, within those objects themselves.

But what of the rose? Its appearance as the subject of the last poem is prepared for earlier in the sequence, and the preparation itself is extremely subtle. Only in the first poem are we told explicitly of the rose's significance: "The rose exceeds, the rose exceeds us all"; and in the same poem he speaks of "The eye quiet on the growing rose/ . . . the imperishable quiet at the heart of form." We are aware from the outset that Roethke seeks in the rose a permanence and stability that he must deny the self if he is to realize the potential inherent in the soul. But were he to continue to stress the value of stasis, the journey out of the self could not proceed; and so references to the rose are discontinued after the first poem. Quietly, though, flowers in general are associated with the water in "Journey to the Interior," and in the conjunction of the two they become at once fluid and static, individual and universal.

> I see the flower of all water, above and below me, the never receding,
> Moving, unmoving in a parched land, white in the moonlight:
> The soul at a still-stand,
> At ease after rocking the flesh to sleep,
> Petals and reflections of petals mixed on the surface of a glassy pool,
> And the waves flattening out when the fisherman drag their nets
>   over the stones.

In "The Long Waters," it is light as well as water that suggests the flowers: "These waves, in the sun, remind me of flowers."

Whatever value the figurative stability of the rose is to possess, Roethke insists that it can be experienced only with a simultaneous commitment to the literal transiency of the other. And so before he tells us, in Section 2 of "The Rose," that "this rose, this rose in the seawind,/ Stays," he describes the journey out of the self in detail that represents most of the categories of the hierarchy.

> I sway outside myself
> Into the darkening currents,
> Into the small spillage of driftwood,
> The waters swirling past the tiny headlands.
> Was it here I wore a crown of birds for a moment
> While on a far point of the rocks
> The light heightened,
> And below, in a mist out of nowhere,
> The first rain gathered?

But once the rose has been engaged on the transcendent terms which he attributes to it, he reconstructs a memory of his childhood and his father.

> And I think of roses, roses,
> White and red, in the wide six-hundred-foot greenhouses,
> And my father standing astride the cement benches,
> Lifting me high over the four-foot stems, the Mrs. Russells,
>   and his own elaborate hybrids,
> And how those flowerheads seemed to flow toward me, to beckon
>   me, only a child, out of myself.
>
> What need for heaven, then,
> With that man, and those roses?

He acknowledges the rose and his earthly father as the first of his mediators. His memory of them encloses his journey out of the self and thus represents for him the totality of the experience. The memory leads him to catalogue intensely particular sounds of North America. Collectively, and in their beauty, these sounds evoke for him "that sound, that single sound,/ When the mind remembers all,/ And gently the light enters the sleeping soul." As he thinks of the "light making its own silence," light, silence, and their more palpable corollary the rose, imply the totality to which he was led in seeking the nothing. As long as he was alive, so long was his mind with him, thus insuring his infinite separation from the other. But there resided in his desire to close that distance a sensitivity and articulateness that enabled him to define with great power one of the central dilemmas of the human condition.

David Ferry

Roethke's Poetry

There are many things wrong with the poetry of Theodore Roethke, things which become the more troubling when one reads him in this collected edition. His seriousness is frequently too solemnly serious, his lyrical qualities too lyrically lyrical. His mystical vein often seems willed, forced, even made up for the occasion, as if it were one with a desire to write that sort of poem. (I am not suggesting that Roethke's feelings were not genuine in this regard. I am speaking only of their expression in his poems.) The love poetry is frequently embarrassing:

> I knew a woman, lovely in her bones,
> When small birds sighed, she would sigh back at them;
> Ah, when she moved, she moved more ways than one:
> The shapes a bright container can contain!
> Of her choice virtues only gods should speak,
> Or English poets who grew up on Greek
> (I'd have them sing in chorus, cheek to cheek).

Too often he permits himself a kind of strident bullying ebullience which is unconvincing and distasteful:

> An exultation takes us outside life:
> I can delight in my own hardihood;
> I taste my sister when I kiss my wife;
> I drink good liquor when my luck is good.
>
> A drunkard drinks, and belches in his drink;
> Such ardor tames eternity, I think.

This kind of thing is especially unconvincing and distasteful because it is so at odds with what is best in his poetry.

Also, there is the dangerous temptation for him of the end-stopped line, a formal obsession of his, which sometimes, to be sure, results in effective and distinctive writing but which nevertheless much of the time is self-crippling and self-baffling. There are poems constructed almost entirely of such lines, but one can see, even in a stanza where it occurs but once, how in his hands it

From *The Virginia Quarterly Review,* XLIII (Winter 1967), 169-73. Reprinted by permission of the author and *The Virginia Quarterly Review.*

can lead to an effect of glibness and quite irrelevant and unintended jaunti-
ness, killing an otherwise interesting stanza:

> Godhead above my God, are you there still?
> To sleep is all my life. In sleep's half-death,
> My body alters, altering the soul
> That once could melt the dark with its small breath.
> Lord, hear me out, and hear me out this day.

There are times when some of his impulses are quite simply disastrous,
occurring as they do in poems in which there is at the same time so much
power, as in "The Renewal," with its impressive penultimate stanza:

> Sudden renewal of the self—from where?
> A raw ghost drinks the fluid in my spine;
> I know I love, yet know not where I am;
> I paw the dark, the shifting midnight air.
> Will the self, lost, be found again? In form?
> I walk the night to keep my five wits warm.

which is ruined by the stridently asserted affirmation of the concluding
stanza:

> Dry bones! Dry bones! I find my loving heart,
> Illumination brought to such a pitch
> I see the rubblestones begin to stretch
> As if reality had split apart
> And the whole motion of the soul lay bare:
> I find that love, and I am everywhere.

Perhaps only the Yeats of "Among School Children" was capable of bringing
off that sort of affirmation successfully. In any case, I think Roethke fails to
do so, and the failure is the more lamentable because the poem had promised
to be the successful expression of feelings of a rather different, a more complex and more limited kind. Very often, in such poems as this, a dazzle of
exaltation falls across them which almost always seems, to me at least, to be a
falsification of their genuine natures, of the more limited and interesting
thing they were becoming. Roethke asks, in "The Sequel," "Was I too glib
about eternal things?" and the answer must be that sometimes he was, and he
was so partly because he was not in these poems stylistically his own man,
but Yeats's, and partly because such effects as the last stanza of "The
Renewal" seem resolutions too easy for the situations they are meant to
resolve.

And yet Roethke is a very interesting and important poet. For one thing
there is the valuable formal experimentation of the poems which comprise

Praise to the End! (as well as the last section of *The Lost Son and Other Poems* and the first poems in *The Waking*), the brilliance there with which he uses imitations of children's voices, nursery rhymes, his beautiful sense of the lives of small creatures, the shifting rhythms and stanza forms which in these poems serve his purposes with wonderful appropriateness:

> A deep dish. Lumps in it.
> I can't taste my mother.
> Hoo. I know the spoon.
> Sit in my mouth.

Or:

> Sing, sing, you symbols! All simple creatures,
> All small shapes, willow-shy,
> In the obscure haze, sing!
>
> A light song comes from the leaves.
> A slow sigh says yes. And light sighs;
> A low voice, summer-sad.
> Is it you, cold father? Father,
> For whom the minnows sang?

Single quotations don't help much here in demonstrating what he is doing and with what degree of success, a good deal of the effect residing as it does in the shifts and changes as the poems go on. Read as a whole, however, the poems of this period of his career give us the sense that something genuinely new and genuinely daring was being attempted. Mr. Karl Malkoff, in his *Theodore Roethke: An Introduction to the Poetry,* is expecially helpful in his elucidation of these particular poems, though I must confess that they don't in the end seem utterly and authoritatively coherent. It is the attempt that is interesting, and the kinds of life that come into the poet's voice in making the attempt.

Then there are also a few poems ("The Adamant," "The Premonition," "The Light Comes Brighter," "The Reminder") from the first book, *Open House,* nearly all of the second, *The Lost Son and Other Poems,* and certain poems from later volumes of the fifties, for example "Elegy for Jane," "A Light Breather," "The Waking," "Old Lady's Winter Words," "Meditations of an Old Woman"—especially the first of these meditations. Their tendency, generally speaking, is to be far more concrete and far more limited in their intentions than some of his other work. And they demonstrate qualities of tenderness, delicacy, fineness of observation very different from some of the qualities for which I have criticized him earlier. He is willing in these to put aside the impulses in his poetic nature which made for stridency, for rhetorical assertiveness of the wrong kind, for spiritual victories which seem—though they were undoubtedly not so for him in his life—too easy in some of his poems. Part I of "The Visitant" is an example of the kind of delicacy and quietness, the rightness of rhythm, which I admire so much in him:

> A cloud moved close. The bulk of the wind shifted.
> A tree swayed over water.
> A voice said:
> Stay. Stay by the slip-ooze. Stay.
>
> Dearest tree, I said, may I rest here?
> A ripple made a soft reply.
> I waited, alert as a dog.
> The leech clinging to a stone waited;
> And the crab, the quiet breather.

And in the last book he published, *The Far Field,* there are signs, for example in "Meditation at Oyster River," of a new and promising expansiveness and tentativeness, a new watchfulness and patience with respect to his experience, and forms of speech appropriate to these qualities. For the reader, the pity is not to be able to see where this would have taken him.

It will not be surprising that Mr. Malkoff in his book has a very different view from mine of the nature of Roethke's accomplishment, at least in many important respects. The book is a careful and patient chronological account of the poems and of Roethke's poetic development. It contains much useful information and it is in general extremely helpful. I also found it in some ways humorless and labored; but also intelligent, an honest and honorable work.

William Heyen

The Divine Abyss: Theodore Roethke's Mysticism

I

It was ever Theodore Roethke's experience that out of personal suffering could issue illumination and genuine poetry. He lived dangerously close to the madness that always threatened to destroy his career as poet and teacher, but such tension was fortunate for Roethke the artist, and the reader of his *Collected Poems* gains a strong impression that the poet realized this. Roethke saw himself as standing at the brink of an abyss, and during the course of his poetry this image becomes symbolic of man's condition. The speakers of his poems often exist in a state of doubt and agony bordering on total despair. But Roethke, in Arnold Stein's terms, cultivated the edge of the abyss, and the creative act held him together.[1]

In "Song" his speaker declares: "The edge is what we have."[2] This theme is often repeated in Roethke. The personae of other poems move toward love, understanding, and happiness, if transiently, after standing perilously close to and looking out over an abyss. The substance of this abyss, this "dark time," is the fear of personal extinction and the horror of alienation in a world in which the individual has lost communion with any transcendental reality. Roethke's own experience with this abyss led to intimations of the divine and to momentary reconciliations of what in "Her Becoming" (*CP*, 166) he calls "... the cold fleshless kiss of contraries." His later poems, especially, make manifest the idea that the deepest gulfs of the soul are illuminated when one journeys out of the superficial self to the interior self, to the true self that when once awakened has the ability to commune with God. Hence Roethke can say, without recoiling in fear, "I live near the abyss, I hope to stay/ Until my eyes look at a brighter sun ..." ("The Pure Fury," *CP*, 134). Indeed, the divine abyss becomes for Roethke a symbol of man's fortunate fall. The man who experiences the edge, "The edge of heaven ... sharper than a sword ..." ("The Tranced," *CP*, 237), and comes away chastened can perceive "The sun! The sun! And all we can become!" ("What Can I Tell My Bones?" *CP*, 173).

From *Texas Studies in Literature and Language,* XI (Winter 1969), 1051-68. Reprinted by permission of *Texas Studies in Literature and Language.*
[1] *Theodore Roethke: Essays on the Poetry,* ed. Arnold Stein (Seattle, 1965), pp. ix-xix. See also R. B. Heilman, "Theodore Roethke: Personal Notes," *Shenandoah,* XVI (Autumn 1964), 55-64.
[2] *The Collected Poems of Theodore Roethke* (New York, 1966), p. 258. Subsequent quotations from Roethke's poems are from this edition, hereafter designated as *CP.*

In *Mysticism: A Study of Man's Spiritual Consciousness,* Evelyn Underhill calls attention to the fact that the great mystics in the Christian tradition felt a sense of communion with the divine during their contemplations of personal voids of darkness. She discusses the growth of ". . . the mystics, who, having completely drunk, have attained the power of gazing into the abyss of the infinite light divine."[3] There is much evidence that Roethke was drawn to Underhill's brilliant study, that to a large extent this book shed light on his personal experiences and shaped his poetic conception of mysticism. No doubt he heard news of himself often in this study, news of the pain that is necessary for mystical insight, of the "agonizing periods of impotence and depression, for each violent outburst of creative energy" (Underhill, 383). Karl Malkoff mentions that Stanley Kunitz, who knew the poet well, suggested to him that much of Roethke's raw material on mysticism came from this source.[4] But, more significant, the phrasings and thematic directions of many of Roethke's later poems indicate that he digested and profited from Underhill's study. Kenneth Burke has discussed "Mysticism as a Solution to the Poet's Dilemma";[5] for Roethke, Underhill was a means to a formal understanding of the mystical tradition. That this understanding was an invaluable asset to his art I hope to make clear during the course of this discussion.

I would like at this point, referring to other of Roethke's poems, to consider "The Abyss" (*CP,* 219-222), a poem that serves as a striking summary of Roethke's mysticism, as the fruition of his mystical studies. In no poem is he more indebted to Underhill, in no poem does he so clearly dramatize the mystical journey of the soul from darkness and conflict to divine light and peace.

I should quickly say that I do not wish to declare Roethke a "mystic proper," in Underhill's sense, a man who dedicates his life to educating himself to achieve union with God. Rather, Roethke was an artist who experienced moments of deep religious feeling and almost inexpressible illumination. His choice was not traditional Christianity or atheism, but a reliance upon the mystic perceptions of his own imagination. "In his ability," says Michael Benedikt, "to meditate convincingly upon the mystical realities of natural existence, in seizing the unseen, Roethke has few parallels among poets in English."[6]

Early in *The Idea of the Holy* Rudolf Otto asks his reader to go no further if he cannot recollect such mystical moments when the existence of the

---

[3]Cleveland, 1965, p. 237. Underhill's study was first published in 1910. Pagination for subsequent quotations given in text.

[4]*Theodore Roethke: An Introduction to the Poetry* (New York, 1966), p. 168.

[5]In *Spiritual Problems in Contemporary Literature,* ed. Stanley Romaine Hopper (New York, 1957), pp. 95-115.

[6]"The Completed Pattern," *Poetry: A Magazine of Verse,* CIX (January 1967), 266.

"wholly other" seems beyond dispute.[7] These experiences, so difficult to describe, have affinities with Wordsworth's "spots in time" (*The Prelude,* XII, 208), times when communion with a universal spirit leads to a peace beyond understanding.

However, I do not wish to understate the formal or traditional mystical content of Roethke's poems. Underhill makes it clear that the "mystic way" can be described in steps only arbitrarily divided, that frequently stages of development overlap, but she goes on to analyze what she sees as the five phases of the mystical experience: The Awakening of Self, The Purification of Self, Illumination, The Dark Night of the Soul, Union. William James also sees no absolute delineation of the mystical experience, but does propose "four marks which, when an experience has them, may justify us in calling it mystical . . .": Ineffability, Noetic Quality, Transiency, Passivity.[8] Roethke's five-section poem, "The Abyss," emphasizes James's requirements and parallels Underhill's analyses of the five-step mystic way. Roethke presents in this poem a dramatization of the mystical movement toward, into, and away from the divine abyss, the dark that flames with creative love.

"Optical disturbances, auditions, and the sense of levitation, are . . . frequent physical accompaniments of these shiftings of the level of consciousness . . ." that occur during the process of Awakening, the first phase of mystical progress (Underhill, 186). The speaker of "The Abyss" hears a voice, perhaps a "distinct interior voice" (Underhill, 273), perhaps an exterior voice already the result of mystic intuition, a "transcendental consciousness" (Underhill, 176). A precise identification of this voice is neither possible nor necessary. In the fourth section of the poem a "shade" speaks. Perhaps these voices of the first and fourth sections are identical. In any case, Awakening is largely an ineffable process, and the first section of "The Abyss" is the most obscure of the five.

> Is the stair here?
> Where's the stair?
> 'The stair's right there,
> But it goes nowhere.'
>
> And the abyss? the abyss?
> 'The abyss you can't miss:
> It's right where you are —
> A step down the stair.'

---

[7]New York, 1958, p. 8. Trans. John W. Harvey. Otto's study, which elucidates the same concept of the "divine abyss" under consideration here, was first published in 1923. Pagination for subsequent quotations given in text.

[8]*The Varieties of Religious Experience* (New York, n.d.), pp. 371-372. First published in 1902. Subsequent references, pagination hereafter given in text, are to this edition.

Each time ever
There always is
Noon of failure,
Part of a house.

In the middle of,
Around a cloud,
On top a thistle
The wind's slowing.

It is important to notice that in "The Abyss," as in the mystical process described by Underhill, Awakening begins *in medias res;* the subject's temperament and surroundings, his "apprehensions of a supersensual reality which he could not find yet could not forget; all these have prepared him for it" (Underhill, 179). The second section of "The Abyss," largely a flashback to the personality and environment of the speaker, will do much to illuminate just what it was that spurred the Awakening in these four stanzas. This is not to say, however, that by themselves they are inexplicable.

Roethke immediately places his speaker in a spiritual crisis. The short, choppy lines and the sibilants suggest an almost breathless tension. The voice says that the stair on which the speaker is poised rises to "nowhere," but that the abyss is only a step below. This suggests, then, that to go anywhere at all, the speaker must step downward toward the abyss. The descent into pain and humiliation, the Purgative Way, is anticipated here.

Underhill quotes a poem by St. John of the Cross translated by Arthur Symons, "En Una Noche Escura" (352). Its similarities with Roethke's poem are striking. These are its first two stanzas:

Upon an obscure night
Fevered with Love's anxiety
(O hapless, happy plight!)
I went, none seeing me,
Forth from my house, where all things quiet be.

By night, secure from sight
And by a secret stair, disguisedly,
(O hapless, happy plight!)
By night, and privily
Forth from my house, where all things quiet be.

Here the poet leaves his house (associated in the Christian tradition and in much of Roethke's poetry with the body) to undertake a journey on a dark night. In "The Abyss" the speaker engages in a discussion with a voice (again, perhaps inner) in a house in which there always seems to be "noon" or zenith "of failure." St. John later declares: "That light did lead me on,/ More surely than the shining of noontide. . . ." Light imagery, though most central to the stage of Illumination, constantly accompanies Awakening in the mystic's development (Underhill 179), and the word "noon" in Roethke's poem bears much weight, even if whatever light there is in this case serves to point up "failure." The speaker of "The Abyss" also travels on an obscure night, as we shall see in subsequent sections.

The St. John of the Cross poem describes a journey that took place in the past and one that the poet understands to have been a "hapless, happy plight"; Roethke's speaker will go on in "The Abyss" to describe, in symbolic terms because the experience is virtually inexpressible, the journey toward Illumination and reconciliation of opposites. He now recognizes, however, what we may call the "symptoms" of the approaching moments: "Each time ever" there is a sense of failure as concrete as "Part of a house." This image itself suggests Roethke's constant concern with the "several selves" ("The Exorcism," *CP,* 147) that need to be drawn together.

Roethke's stair is the "secret stair" of the St. John of the Cross poem, a traditional mystical symbol. In order to mount the stair to God, one has first to descend. The stair, its ultimate potential, is always there, but the mystic does not rise directly to Union before pain and Purgation. Roethke was aware of the easy, false kind of mysticism against which Underhill frequently cautions, the "pelludious Jesus-shimmer over all things" of "O, Thou Opening, O" (*CP,* 98). There is no straight ascent to communion. The lover must go a long, dark way. Perhaps the "cloud" of Roethke's final stanza is a reference to the anonymous author of "The Cloud of Unknowing": "By love He may be gotten and holden, but by thought of understanding, never" (Underhill, 48).

In Roethke's poetry a slowing or shifting wind is often ominous, is the hush before the storm, is a time when the self awakens to expectations of it knows not what. Perhaps what is hoped for will not happen:

> The rain stayed in its cloud; full dark came near;
> The wind lay motionless in the long grass.
> The veins within our hands betrayed our fear.
> What we had hoped for had not come to pass.
> ("Interlude," *CP,* 6)

Or perhaps the wind that "creaks slowly by" will pick up and lead the speaker to love ("Words for the Wind," *CP,* 123-126). In "In a Dark Time" (*CP,* 239), at the culmination of mystical contemplation,[9] "one is One, free

---

[9] See Roethke's essay on this poem in *The Contemporary Poet as Artist and Critic: Eight Symposia,* ed. Anthony Ostroff (Boston, 1964), pp. 49-53. Many of Roethke's comments on mysticism echo Underhill's study.

in the tearing wind." The speaker of "I waited" was glad when "all the winds came toward me" (*CP,* 247). In any case, Roethke ends the first section of "The Abyss" with an image of anticipation. The soul of the despairing speaker has, in another dark time, been awakened. The absence of end rhyme in the last stanza, after twelve lines employing, altogether, just two different rhymes, may also suggest that the speaker has readied himself to experience a new way of saying, hearing, and seeing.

II

During the second phase of the mystic's development, Purification, the newly awakened self feels a deep necessity to replace, with a new reality, what has been its false and superficial existence (Underhill, 198-231). This stage involves a humiliation of self and a purgation. The "secret stair" leads downward. Underhill defines "Mortification," central to Purification, as "a deliberate recourse to painful experiences and difficult tasks" (205). In the second section of "The Abyss" the speaker's mortification is introspection: he faces himself with the fact that, according to any sense of meaningful values, he has been living an unlife.

> I have been spoken to variously
> But heard little.
> My inward witness is dismayed
> By my unguarded mouth.
> I have taken, too often, the dangerous path,
> The vague, the arid,
> Neither in nor out of this life.
>
> Among us, who is holy?
> What speech abides?
> I hear the noise of the wall.
> They have declared themselves,
> Those who despise the dove.
>
> Be with me, Whitman, maker of catalogues:
> For the world invades me again,
> And once more the tongues begin babbling.
> And the terrible hunger for objects quails me:
> The sill trembles.
> And there on the blind
> A furred caterpillar crawls down a string.
> My symbol!
> For I have moved closer to death, lived with death;
> Like a nurse he sat with me for weeks, a sly surly attendant,
> Watching my hands, wary.
> Who sent him away?

> I'm no longer a bird dipping a beak into rippling water
> But a mole winding through earth,
> A night-fishing otter.

Here the speaker engages in self-criticism. He realizes that often his "un-guarded mouth" dismays his true self, that he has taken a "dangerous path," one "vague" and "arid," neither inward nor outward to true being. He realizes that the world of the senses, the material world, means too much to him. The mystics, says Underhill, achieve a poverty of the senses. They regard "cravings which are excited by different aspects of the phenomenal world . . . as gross infringements of the law of love" (Underhill, 220). "Is there a wisdom in objects? Few objects praise the Lord" ("Her Becoming," *CP,* 166). That this "terrible hunger for objects quails" the speaker of "The Abyss" is a sign of mortification. In his essay "On 'Identity' " Roethke sums up what for him is a recurrent theme: we make "a fetish of 'thing-hood,' we surround ourselves with junk, ugly objects. . . ."[10]

Roethke begins the second stanza with two rhetorical questions. Certainly, none among us is holy and no speech abides. Those who declare the opposite "despise the dove" of peace, the dove of the "inward witness," of the Holy Ghost. This is the world of superficiality and hate that in the third stanza "invades" the speaker with its babbling tongues. We may associate the "noise of the wall" with the "Part of a house" in the first part of the poem and the idea of failure.

"There are some areas of experience in modern life," says Roethke in "Some Remarks on Rhythm," "that simply cannot be rendered by either the formal lyric or straight prose. We need the catalogue in our time" (*SP,* 83). From its second section on, "The Abyss" is rendered in free verse; Whitman is Roethke's prime "spiritual father" here, not Yeats, whose ghost is always present in Roethke's formal lyrics of *The Waking* and *Words for the Wind.*

The vital Whitman of the catalogue, the Whitman of love and transcendental faith, who declares, in "Song of Myself," "The wonder is always and always how there can be a mean man or an infidel," the Whitman who happily contradicts himself, is invoked by the speaker as a bulwark against objects and the babbling tongues (the tongues of Babel) of the world. Whitman also often makes the long journey out of self, becoming in "Song of Myself," for example, a ship's captain and an artillerist. Both Underhill and James acknowledge Whitman's mystical qualities, and in "The Abyss," through his speaker, Roethke calls on Whitman as a symbol of the poet who achieves spiritual salvation through his efforts to strike out for the real world, the world that gives substance and true speech to the world of sensation.

---

[10]*On the Poet and His Craft: Selected Prose of Theodore Roethke,* ed. Ralph J. Mills, Jr. (Seattle, 1965), pp. 19-20. Hereafter designated as *SP.*

At one moment Whitman expresses his love for all humanity, and at the next moment wishes to murder a man he despises. He sees himself as an organism of contradictions, but is at peace with himself in a way that defies reason and the essentially false precision of learned astronomers. Roethke can also call reason "That dreary shed, that hutch for grubby schoolboys!" ("I Cry, Love! Love!" *CP,* 92). He can say "When I raged, when I wailed,/ And my reason failed,/ That delicate thing my soul/ Grew back a new wing" ("The Restored," *CP,* 249). And rational thought is never, as Underhill makes abundantly clear, an innate part of mystical progress. The mystical Whitman, too, then, is the Whitman called upon here; the poet who sounds what James describes as "depths of truth unplumbed by the discursive intellect" (371). Roethke will turn more explicitly to the mystic's manner of "knowing" in the fourth section of "The Abyss."

In a sense Whitman always realizes what the speaker in Roethke's poem discovers: the caterpillar, having the potential to grow wings and be a creature of beauty, is a symbol of the self. But as a creature of Becoming rather than Being it must first experience a dark and grounded time. It is on the string of a "blind" and is moving "down," just as the speaker must descend on the secret stair. The mystic is a constant seeker of symbols, and Roethke's speaker declares that he has found his.

The speaker here is more than a little amazed that he escaped death, and wonders who sent him away. This is an expression of awe, of what Otto calls the "numinous raw material for the feeling of religious humility" (20) in the face of the "wholly other," which *does* abide. And the humility here, which comes after the recognition of personal sin and falsehood, is the primary requisite for the purification of self.

Emphasizing this humility and purification are the contrasted bird and mole-otter images of the final stanza. The dazzling thing of the air becomes a night-fisher, a creature of the ground that hunts its sustenance in the dark. The speaker has first to degrade himself, for "A man goes far to find out what he is . . ." ("In a Dark Time," *CP,* 239); "From me to Thee's a long and terrible way" ("The Marrow," *CP,* 246). The "mole winding" through earth and the "night-fishing otter" are appropriate symbols, with the caterpillar, of purgation, quest, and hope. Though death, for the moment, has been sent away, the speaker is still on the mystic stairway of introspection and needs to descend. Underhill, discussing the spiritual and material Poverty necessary to Purification, adequately sums up the movement of the second section of "The Abyss":

> Poverty, then, prepares man's spirit for that union with God to which it aspires. She strips off the clothing which he so often mistakes for himself, transvaluates all his values, and shows him things as they are. (208)

III

In the third part of "The Abyss" Roethke explores the descent into Illumination and its consequences. If, to this point, there have been insights into the falseness of the superficial self, subsequent insights will reveal the transcendent reality inherent in the world. Underhill describes the Illumination of Self as "the great swing back into sunshine which is the reward of that painful descent into the 'cell of self-knowledge' " (233). Here the moment of the abyss, at first too real and fearful—a "blinding misery"—is perceived as a moment of peace, but only when the speaker waits courageously and displays that paradoxical active passivity described by Underhill and the Christian mystics.

> Too much reality can be a dazzle, a surfeit;
> Too close immediacy an exhaustion:
> As when the door swings open in a florist's storeroom—
> The rush of smells strikes like a cold fire, the throat freezes,
> And we turn back to the heat of August,
> Chastened.
>
> So the abyss—
> The slippery cold heights,
> After the blinding misery,
> The climbing, the endless turning,
> Strike like a fire,
> A terrible violence of creation,
> A flash into the burning heart of the abominable;
> Yet, if we wait, unafraid, beyond the fearful instant,
> The burning lake turns into a forest pool,
> The fire subsides into rings of water,
> A sunlit silence.

During the mystic's journey, Underhill tells us, Illumination tends to manifest itself in three ways: (1) "A joyous apprehension of the Absolute"; (2) a clarity of perception, a heightening of vision concerning the phenomenal world; (3) an increase of the "energy of the intuitional or transcendental self" (240). Reality, the Absolute, is a complex of contraries that merge. The self, perceiving the true nature of the abyss, is here utilizing its energy of intuition, but also apparent here is the "Passivity" to which mystics point, for the speaker says that we need only wait (after the awakening and purgation) for the "sunlit silence" of Illumination: "When the characteristic sort of consciousness once has set in, the mystic feels as if his own will were in abeyance, and indeed sometimes as if he were grasped and held by a superior power" (James 372).

As Underhill and the mystics with whom she deals consistently say, the moment of Illumination is inexpressible except in symbolic terms. In the third section of "The Abyss" the speaker falls back on a "florist's storeroom" in his effort to describe indescribable experience. He has experienced something of the descent into the abyss in the intense smells that strike like "cold fire."

In an uncollected poem, "Song" (*Poetry*, CV, Oct.-Nov. 1963, 87), Roethke uses as his epigraph Underhill's "This fragrance, as St. Augustine calls it . . ." (331). Before using these words Underhill quotes from St. Augustine, who describes a sudden onrush of "sensuous images" during one of his moments of Illumination:

> . . . but I could not sustain my gaze: my weakness was dashed back, and I was relegated to my ordinary experience, bearing with me only a loving memory, and as it were the fragrance of those desirable meats on the which as yet I was not able to feed. (331)

In "The Abyss" the smells themselves are intimations of the Absolute, but the speaker is not yet ready for Union and turns back, as does Augustine. "Too much reality can be a dazzle, a surfeit. . . ." Roethke's use of Underhill here and in "Song" is an indication of just how closely he read her book. He fastens on terminology that has, no doubt, after his greenhouse childhood, a great deal of meaning for him, and adapts it to his dramatization of the developing mystical consciousness of his speaker.

The speaker falls back on the oxymoron, as have so many mystics, to represent the awful contraries of the journey, to apprehend simultaneity: smells strike like a "cold fire"; the abyss is composed of "heights"; the lake burns. He returns from the cold of the storeroom to the heat of August chastened as he returns from the "slippery cold" of the abyss to the sunlight and Illumination of the moments following. All creation is suddenly understood to be a "violence" which yokes together what were before irreconcilable opposites for the self. But there must first be a "blinding misery," a "climbing" and "endless turning," before "The burning lake turns into a forest pool. . . ." Roethke's imagery is very similar to Underhill's: ". . . the Finite slowly approaches the nature of its Infinite Source: climbing up the cleansing mountain pool by pool . . . until it reaches its Origin" (204).

That light is the essence of the heart of darkness is an idea frequently declared by Roethke's speakers: In "O, Thou Opening, O" (*CP*, 98) "The dark has its own light"; in "Praise to the End!" "The dark showed me a face" (*CP*, 88). Underhill quotes Maurice Maeterlinck's description of the moment of the abyss: "we stand suddenly at the confines of human thought, and far beyond the polar circle of the mind. It is intensely cold here; it is intensely dark; and yet you will find nothing but flames and light" (340).

Roethke makes frequent use of flame imagery in his poetry, often, as he does here, to express the reconcilable contraries of experience. Though it burns to ashes, "A log sings in its flame" ("Love's Progress," *CP,* 137). In the same poem the speaker tells us he "would drown in fire." At the shore in "The Long Waters" "My body shimmers with a light flame" (*CP,* 198). "Such fire imagery has seemed to many of the mystics a peculiarly exact and suggestive symbol of the transcendent state which they are struggling to describe" (Underhill, 421).

In section three of "The Abyss" the phrase "beyond the fearful instant" is important. The mystic gradually escapes the world of flux, the world of Becoming, of time, to merge with the reality that is eternal. In "The Rose" (*CP,* 205) Roethke writes: "And I stood outside myself,/ Beyond becoming and perishing,/ A something wholly other. . . ." It is this time beyond the fearful, this stasis beyond the perspective of the dying and false body that Roethke's speaker achieves, if only momentarily, during his phase of Illumination in "The Abyss." He has just attained a moment of peace. The fire of the abyss "subsides into rings of water,/ A sunlit silence." Two things are noticeable in this conclusion. We are again reminded of the "bird dipping a beak into rippling water" of the second section of the poem; here the suggestion is that the deep and dark mole-otter journey is temporarily over. And we notice the subsiding, the stasis, the still point during the moments after the speaker divines the true nature of the abyss. This quiet and freedom from time is important if the final end of the journey, mystical union with the absolute, is to be achieved. Underhill quotes Meister Eckhart:

> He must be in a stillness and silence, where the Word may be heard. One cannot draw near to this Word better than by stillness and silence. . . . And when we simply keep ourselves receptive, we are more perfect than when at work. (319)

Hence the traveler says we must "wait, unafraid. . . ."

Critics have charged that Roethke, unlike Yeats or Wallace Stevens, does not earn his affirmation, that there has been too little spiritual wrestling, that in many poems, a condition of joy arises artificially and without preparation.[11] These charges are not without some foundation, but it is important to realize that the happiness achieved in any Roethke poem, and this will become apparent in "The Abyss," is not one based on reason, on step-by-step logical confrontations with dissatisfaction, on rational duels with and

---

[11]See, for example, M. L. Rosenthal, *The Modern Poets* (New York, 1965), pp. 243-244; David Ferry, "Roethke's Poetry," *Virginia Quarterly Review,* XLIII (Winter 1967), 171; also Denis Donoghue, "Roethke's Broken Music," *Theodore Roethke: Essays on the Poetry,* ed. Arnold Stein (Seattle, 1965), pp. 141-142.

victories over disquieting thoughts. The movement of most Roethke poems is comparable to that of the fourth section of Yeats's "Vacillation" in which joy is sudden and the realization of happiness is logically unfounded, is intuitive:

> My fiftieth year had come and gone,
> I sat, a solitary man,
> In a crowded London shop,
> An open book and empty cup
> On the marble table-top.
>
> While on the shop and street I gazed
> My body of a sudden blazed;
> And twenty minutes more or less
> It seemed, so great my happiness,
> That I was blessèd and could bless.[12]

This movement is unusual in the body of Yeats's work, but the same sudden leap from pain to joy is frequently apparent in Roethke. One of the reasons that several of Roethke's mystical lyrics of *Words for the Wind* and especially *The Far Field* are so successful is that the mystical experience itself is ineffable, does not proceed reasonably. And now in the late 1950's and early 1960's, armed with his study of Underhill and the mystics she discusses, Roethke has found his rationale, one he had always suspected to be real, but one that leads to a new confidence and power: he can rock irrationally between dark and light, can go by feeling where he has to go.

IV

After the stage of Illumination he has to go downward. In the fourth section of "The Abyss" Roethke's speaker experiences the next stage in the mystic's growth, the Dark Night of the Soul. We notice, since this stage is akin to Purification, since suffering and purgation are again necessary before Union can occur, that the form of this section is much like that of the second.

> How can I dream except beyond this life?
> Can I outleap the sea—
> The edge of all the land, the final sea?
> I envy the tendrils, their eyeless seeking,
> The child's hand reaching into the coiled smilax,
> And I obey the wind at my back
> Bringing me home from the twilight fishing.

---

[12]*The Collected Poems of W. B. Yeats* (New York, 1961), p. 246.

> In this, my half-rest,
> Knowing slows for a moment,
> And not-knowing enters, silent,
> Bearing being itself,
> And the fire dances
> To the stream's
> Flowing.
>
> Do we move toward God, or merely another condition?
> By the salt waves I hear a river's undersong,
> In a place of mottled clouds, a thin mist morning and evening.
> I rock between dark and dark,
> My soul nearly my own,
> My dead selves singing.
> And I embrace this calm—
> Such quiet under the small leaves!—
> Near the stem, whiter at root,
> A luminous stillness.
>
> The shade speaks slowly:
> 'Adore and draw near.
> Who knows this—
> Knows all.'

One of the chief characteristics of mystical development, as Underhill often reiterates, is a "series of oscillations" between periods of pleasure and pain. During the Dark Night the self "is tossed back from its hard-won point of vantage." Doubt, acute feelings of imperfection, and "an overwhelming sense of darkness and deprivation" are common to this stage (Underhill, 382). The Dark Night, says Underhill, "must entail bitter suffering: far worse than that endured in the Purgative way" (389).

Of the five sections of "The Abyss" the fourth seems, at first, to be farthest from paralleling the five-step Mystic Way. Roethke does not seem to emphasize intense suffering here. His speaker is being brought home from the otter's journey of section two, "home from the twilight fishing." This in itself suggests that he is nearing the end of his quest. But what is the suffering of decades for the mystic is likely to result in melodrama in a poem the length of "The Abyss"; nevertheless, if Roethke's voice is artfully subdued, there are suggestions in this section of the mental anguish, despair, and finally the heroic resignation in the face of this anguish and despair of the speaker. He says that he is still only at "half-rest," that he rocks between "dark and dark. . . ." He says that his soul is only "nearly my own," and there is no more frightening possibility for Roethke, as Karl Malkoff testifies, than the possibility that mystical Union might entail total loss of self-identity.[13] The

---

[13]Malkoff, p. 173.

speaker also suggests his willingness to accept serenity without knowledge. All these details point to a quiet desperation, but one, from the poet's point of view, that does not risk melodrama or sentimentality.

We notice in the first stanza that though he envies what he feels he cannot be, the speaker obeys. Until the shade speaks, the traveler is puzzled by the peace he feels. But he has earned the right, without knowing it, to draw near and adore. Underhill cautions: "We must remember in the midst of our analysis, that the mystic life is a life of love: that the Object of the mystic's final quest and of his constant intuition is an object of adoration . . ." (389).

At the beginning of the section the speaker sees himself at the "edge," at the line of demarcation between this life, the land, and a sea that is "final" or ultimate. He wonders whether or not he can "outleap" what he envisions as eternal death to reach some farther place. He envies the "eyeless seeking" of tendrils and we are reminded of many greenhouse poems and of "A Light Breather" (*CP*, 101) in which the spirit moves "in the light with its tendrils. . . ." In "Cuttings (later)" (*CP*, 37) Roethke asks: "What saint strained so much,/ Rose on such lopped limbs to a new life?" Tendrils are beginnings. They seek, and unquestioningly, courageously, take hold on their new reality.

Soon "not-knowing," a kind of "eyeless seeking," enters, and bears just "being itself. . . ." Underhill makes it clear that mystical "knowing" is itself a paradox, that we use the word only because no other is available. In the mystical sense, knowing is not limited to "sense impressions, . . . to any process of intellection, . . . to the unfolding of the content of normal consciousness" (Underhill, 23-24). The mystic knows "As a blind man, lifting a curtain, knows it is morning . . ." ("Journey to the Interior," *CP*, 195). In "The Manifestation" (*CP*, 235) Roethke's speaker concludes: "We come to something without knowing why." The speaker of "The Abyss" has reached the point at which he feels he knows nothing. Paradoxically, but in a mystical sense logically, the shade will tell him that he "knows all." During moments of contemplation the soul of the mystic learns "the world's secret, not by knowing, but by being: the only way of really knowing anything" (Underhill, 342). Opposites become part of the mystic's achieved harmony: "And the fire dances/ To the stream's/ Flowing." This is the "great stream of spiritual life" Underhill mentions (399).

But the wavelike oscillation of mystical progress again intrudes. The speaker asks a disturbing question: "Do we move toward God, or merely another condition?" "Delacroix," writes Underhill,

> after an . . . analysis of St. Teresa's progress towards Union with the Absolute, ends upon the assumption that the God with whom she was united was the content of her own subconscious mind. (14)

This is the speaker's skeptical question. Is he truly, after Awakening, Purification, and Illumination, moving "toward God," or is he moving to merely another "condition" of self? But he soon, instinctively or intuitively rather than rationally, rocks away from this question; he hears a "river's undersong. . . ." And, not to be denied, his dead selves sing. In traditional mystical terminology, he dies that he may live. He reaches calm again.

The self that still lives learns that there is "Near the stem, whiter at root,/ A luminous stillness." The speaker moves to the stasis that he achieved at the conclusion of the stage of Illumination. Underhill uses the phrase "luminous darkness" (249). Again, as with "sunlit silence," Roethke employs light imagery to describe that moment of quiet when his speaker feels nearest God.

The shade uses the referent "this": " 'Who knows this—/ Knows all.' " The speaker has just perceived the significance of something he had probably always known: at the root the stem is whiter. So it is with the abyss. One must descend into darkness, the Divine Abyss, to experience the grandeur of God that will, in Hopkins's words, "flame out, like shining from shook foil. . . ."

V

In the final section of "The Abyss" Roethke's speaker experiences Union, the fifth stage of the Mystic Way and "the true goal of the mystic quest" (Underhill, 170). Discussing the Unitive Life, Underhill differentiates between two mystical ways of apprehending God:

> (1) The metaphysical mystic, for whom the Absolute is impersonal and transcendent, describes his final attainment of that Absolute as *deification*, or the utter transmutation of the self in God. (2) The mystic for whom intimate and personal communion has been the mode under which he best apprehended Reality, speaks of the consummation of this communion, its perfect and permanent form, as the *Spiritual Marriage* of his soul with God. (415)

The speaker of "The Abyss" seeks personal communion, "marriage." The self is not utterly lost, annihilated, but maintains its own identity during communion. Nine times the word "I" in this section declares this.

> I thirst by day. I watch by night.
> I receive! I have been received!
> I hear the flowers drinking in their light,
> I have taken counsel of the crab and the sea-urchin,
> I recall the falling of small waters,
> The stream slipping beneath the mossy logs,
> Winding down to the stretch of irregular sand,
> The great logs piled like matchsticks.

> I am most immoderately married:
> The Lord God has taken my heaviness away;
> I have merged, like the bird, with the bright air,
> And my thought flies to the place by the bo-tree.
>
> Being, not doing, is my first joy.

Perhaps it is this avowal of selfhood that explains the speaker's "immoderate" marriage. In "On 'Identity' " (*SP*, 26) Roethke says: "I can't claim that the soul, my soul, was absorbed in God during mystical illumination. No, God for me still remains someone to be confronted, to be dueled with: . . . But the oneness, Yes!" The mystic's soul becomes "an abyss of receptivity . . ." (Underhill, 320). The speaker here receives and is received, draws near and is drawn. In much the same way Roethke declares in "The Marrow," maintaining identity to the end, "Yes, I have slain my will, and still I live" (*CP*, 246).

Union, in one sense a state of the highest illumination, is accompanied by an increased perception. The speaker can hear "flowers drinking in their light. . . ." The mystics Underhill studies often refer to their desire for perfection, their desire to commune with God, as a "thirst." The first line in this section suggests that the speaker is willing to accept the pain and uncertainty that will continue to accompany mystical progress. He is also willing to take counsel of two small creatures (including the crab, for Roethke a tireless creature of spiritual becoming) of that sea which has already been established as a symbol of death, but a death that can be transcended. "Night" and "light," the only two full rhymes of the section, convey what continues to be the paradoxical mystery of mysticism, "luminous darkness."

If reminiscence in the second section of "The Abyss" is painful, here the speaker's realization is that God was always immanent. He is able to recall a waterfall, "the falling of small waters." His path is not "arid." Logs are piled like matchsticks, ready to burst into flame. The "stream" of the first stanza of this section seems to lead him to the shore, the "edge of all the land. . . ."

In "Cuttings (later)" (*CP*, 37), "The Long Alley" (*CP*, 61), and "Fourth Meditation" (*CP*, 168) Roethke associates "small waters" with resurrection, with new life, as he does in "The Abyss." And as the speaker of "The Sententious Man" says, "water moves until it's purified . . ." (*CP*, 132); standing water in Roethke, on the other hand, is "privy to oily fungus and . . . algae . . ." ("Unfold! Unfold!" *CP*, 89), is suggestive of spiritual stagnation.

God has taken away the "heaviness" that drew the caterpillar down the string and the mole and otter on their journeys. Now, like a bird, the traveler merges with the "bright air. . . ." The mystics often use bird imagery to describe their feelings of transcendence during Union. The soul "flies high" (Underhill, 427) just as the speaker's "thought flies to the place by the bo-tree . . ." where Buddha received enlightenment.

In this final and climactic section, then, the speaker declares his Union, his marriage, with the divine; his journey has reached fruition. Mystical union, as Underhill points out, is a culmination of love, rapture, and Illumination. Roethke sums this up in his last line: "Being, not doing, is my first joy." Underhill writes: "Being, not Doing, is the first aim of the mystic . . ." (380). "Being" is to leave the world of constant flux, the world of becoming, the world of time.

I hope that I have suggested, during the course of this paper, that in Underhill's terms the mystic's journey is the essence of many of Roethke's later poems. Throughout his career Roethke was sympathetic with the mystic's point of view, but only in his later work does he bulwark his intimations of mysticism with a formal understanding of its tradition. The voice of Underhill's description of the Mystic Way is inescapable in "The Renewal," "Love's Progress," "Plaint," "The Song," "The Small," "A Walk in Late Summer," and "Meditations of an Old Woman" of *Words for the Wind;* the same is true of "North American Sequence," "The Manifestation," "The Tranced," "The Moment," "In a Dark Time," "In Evening Air," "The Sequel," "The Motion," "Infirmity," "The Marrow," and "The Tree, The Bird," of *The Far Field.* If "The Abyss" is the prototypical mystical poem in the Roethke canon, all these others presuppose much of the information in Underhill's book that the poet absorbed. It is seldom that a single book sheds so much light on a major portion of a poet's work. Though, certainly, "The Abyss" is not a literary exercise in which Roethke sets out to parallel Underhill, Roethke weaves Underhill into the fabric of his own spiritual life.

Finally, to say that "The Abyss" "obviously dramatizes a bout with madness . . .,"[14] is to simplify its complexity and universality of theme almost to absurdity. In this poem Roethke dramatizes, for an age that has lost its faith, an individual's hard and dark mystic way to God, whose essence he best perceives when he descends into and experiences the true nature of the Divine Abyss.

---

[14]Cleanth Brooks, John Thibaut Purser, and Robert Penn Warren, *An Approach to Literature* (New York, 1964), p. 374. Brooks, in his *Modern Poetry and the Tradition* (New York, 1965), p. xxv, reiterates this narrow conception of "The Abyss."